Seiyu Kiriyama, Founder of Agon Shu Buddhist Association

You Have Been Here Before:
Reincarnation

You Have Been Here Before:

Reincarnation

by

Seiyu Kiriyama

**Founder of Agon Shu
Buddhist Association
Translated by Rande Brown**

HIRAKAWA SHUPPAN INC.

First published in 2000 by
HIRAKAWA SHUPPAN INC.
Mita 3-4-8, Minato-ku, Tokyo 108-0073, Japan

Japanese-English Translation by Rande Brown
In collaboration with
Michiko Abe and Fukiko Kai
Designed by Akihiko Tanimura
Printed and bound in Japan by
NISSHA Printing Co., Ltd.
Paper Supplied by Nakasho, Inc.

Translated from the Japanese original,
first published in 1993 by HIRAKAWA SHUPPAN INC.,
under the title *Kimi wa dare no umarekawari ka.*

Contents

Chapter 1

Reincarnation·········11

On Being a Time Traveler
in the Spiritual Dimensions···87

Chapter 3

What Reincarnates?
The Brain and the Mind········135

Chapter 4

Reincarnation and the Afterworld·········195

Chapter 1

Reincarnation

Szondian Theory and Reincarnation

"I don't believe in things like reincarnation."

"Even if reincarnation is real, it certainly doesn't have anything to do with me or my life."

"I'm too busy to deal with anything like that right now."

Everybody has an opinion.

"But..." I have to interject...

Let's look at some possible scenarios.

What if there is someone who is causing major unhappiness to you personally or to your family as a whole. And what if the reason for the problem is linked to a past life, to reincarnation. Would you be so casual then? Wouldn't you want to understand what is going on?

Or, what if the person you love most in the whole world is actually the reincarnation of someone who committed suicide because of the actions of one of your ancestors? Suppose this person still harbors repressed hostility towards your family and that this hostility is the very thing that impelled him or her to be reborn. And this is what causes the two of you meet, fall in love, and get married.

He or she apparently loves you, but is internally, unconsciously seething with the negativity of the original suicide. It's terrifying to think of what might happen if this negativity should surface. Wouldn't you want as much information about the situation as you could get?

What if you yourself are the negatively driven reincarnate? What would you do then?

As we will see from examining numerous case studies of reincarnation, much suffering in this life is triggered by experiences that happened in a past one.

We will see, further, that in most cases this suffering is not self-contained, but affects other people with whom the given individual is connected.

We will also see that there are many different ways in which reincarnation causes suffering, and that these are not always what one would expect.

For example, although people who are true heroes and geniuses are rare, we occasionally see instances where one of them reincarnates. The fact that they have reincarnated, however, doesn't necessarily mean that the person will be reborn into a circumstance conducive to the expression of his or her gift. The time may not be right to accommodate his or her greatness. For this, or some similar reason, the person will be unable to actualize their potential and this will cause them tremendous pain and frustration.

The situation is exacerbated by the tendency for such talented individuals to be born with stronger characteristics and proclivities than the average person. So when the wind blows against them, their troubles are greater than ordinary people's. Their gifts do not necessarily bring them happiness.

Do you see why you might want to think about all of this? I suggest that it might be worth your while to consider the possibility of reincarnation and the impact that it might be having on you and your life.

I don't mean to alarm you in any way. It's just that I have encountered so many instances where present-day misery is linked to reincarnation that I think it is something we all need to know more about.

I understand that you might not believe in any of this. I will try in the course of this discussion to give you the kind of information that will help convince you of the existence of reincarnation.

Let me begin my argument with an interesting case study. It is something that happened to the famous Hungarian psychoanalyst Dr. Lipot Szondi, a man whose theory of repression opened up new territory in the field of depth psychology as pioneered by Freud and Jung. Szondi experienced something very unusual which I am convinced was related to reincarnation.

Before I describe his experience, let me first try to explain what it is that this great doctor accomplished.

As you know, modern psychology began in 1900 with Freud's theory of psychoanalysis and his contention that we can become conscious of the repressed contents of the mind, the unconscious. This notion forms the basis of depth psychology. This field gradually diverged in two directions according to the layer of mind that was taken as the subject of research.

The first of these directions is that of Freudian psychology, which focuses on the layer of the repressed unconscious of the individual.

The second is that of Jungian psychology, which studies the layer of the repressed unconscious of the collective (1913).

In 1937, Lipot Szondi proposed a third direction, one that takes as its subject of study a layer of consciousness that exists between these other two. This is the stratum of the unconscious mind that Szondi called the 'familial unconscious'. He named his theory of repression concerning this level the theory of fate analysis (*Schicksalsanalyse* in German).

Thus, whereas Freud examined the personal unconscious of the individual and Jung concentrated on the collective unconscious of the group (mass psychology), Szondi decided to focus his study on an intermediate layer of the unconscious that he refers to as the familial unconscious. Szondi discovered the 'family' between the 'individual' of Freud and the 'collective' of Jung.

This provided a unique perspective in the field of depth psychology that has proven to be of enormous use.

Essentially, the theory of fate analysis asserts the following:

The desires of specific ancestors are repressed in the intermediate layer of the unconscious as drives and these drives determine the object choices a person makes in love, friendship, profession, sickness, and possibly even the mode of death.

Szondi contends that there are root factors that we inherit from our ancestors, and that these are what drive our destinies.

This means that the desire patterns of an individual's ancestors are latently encoded in the familial unconsciousness as formations that Szondi calls drives, and that these drives strive to take shape again in the descendants. These drives can exert a determining influence on the choices the individual makes about whom they will love or befriend, what kind of work they will do, how they will get sick, and maybe even on how they die.

At first, this seems like a radically shocking idea. It may even seem like a very frightening one. If it is true, then where is there room for the emergence of an independent self, of a personal identity? It seems totally ridiculous to think that we make a lifetime of choices at the mercy of our ancestors.

Because it's difficult to believe, Szondi went about compiling a staggering number of case histories to prove his point. He was able to amass enough evidence to gain recognition from the scientific community of his time, and his theories are now an accepted line of research in the field. He included many examples from literary giants like Dostoevsky and Balzac in his arguments, and in total his reasoning is very persuasive.

A truly fascinating aspect of all this is that Szondi began to develop his landmark theories from a single unusual experience that he had as a young man. Szondi himself analyzed this experience in the context of depth psychology, but I firmly believe that it had to do more with reincarnation. Let me describe it.

Repetition of the Unhappy Fate of the Ancestors

I've gone ahead and compiled the following version of

Szondi's story from various descriptions of the event that appear in his writings:

> The year is 1916. It is the middle of World War I.
>
> A young military doctor is stationed in Vienna. He is a lieutenant in the army. Every day, he devotedly makes his way to the University to attend the lectures of the renowned psychiatrist Dr. Wagner Georeg.
>
> The young man is in Vienna because he has been assigned to convoy wounded soldiers from his regimental field hospital to the hospital there. He has taken the opportunity afforded by this duty to take a short leave in order to attend the lectures of the esteemed doctor, with whom he has long wanted to study.
>
> When we meet our young lieutenant he is just 23.
>
> He is trying to figure out how to extend his furlough.
>
> He says it's because he wants to spend more time attending the professor's lectures, but that's not the only reason. Soon after arriving in Vienna he met a beautiful, passionate blonde woman and fell madly in love with her. It was his very first time. She is an Aryan girl from Saxony who works as a linguistics teacher. The lieutenant is sure that he wants to marry her. This is the real reason why he wants to stay in Vienna for a while longer.
>
> Then one night he has a disturbing dream.

In the dream his parents are sadly discussing the unhappy fate of his older half-brother.

Thirty years before, his brother was studying medicine at the University of Vienna when he fell in love with a blonde linguistics teacher who was an ethnic Aryan from Saxony.

It is just like what was going on with him!

The scary thing is that everything about the woman he wants to marry is exactly like his brother's girlfriend. She comes from the same place. She looks like her. She even has the same job.

His older half-brother abandoned his plans to take the National Medical Examination in order to marry that woman. The marriage was an utter disaster and the whole affair ended in tragedy. This incident happened before our young doctor was born, and he wasn't clear on the details. He had heard tell of it when he was a child, but it wasn't something he ever thought about.

So why was he having this strange dream now?

The young doctor woke at the first light of dawn with the dream haunting him. He was replaying it over and over in his head when suddenly he felt like he had been struck by lightening.

"What in the world is going on here?"

At that moment he was deeply rocked by a powerful intuition.

This wasn't a coincidence at all!

It was a warning, some kind of sign.

In a flash, it dawns on him that something in

his unconscious mind is compelling him to repeat the fate of his older brother!

But why? He feels desperate to understand the answer. Here he is, a doctor of science with a degree in psychology. He is well versed in the workings of the unconscious. This is the force of the unconscious.

He suddenly becomes terrified that he will repeat the fate of his older half-brother.

He doesn't understand where this drive to repeat his brother's fate is coming from, but he intuitively understands it is something he must resist. He summons all the power of his will and his rationality to fight against this compulsion.

He decides that he must leave Vienna immediately in order to help him sever his overwhelming emotional attachment to the woman. He returns to his regiment that very day.

This is the experience that launched Szondi into his own specialty. This young lieutenant went on to discover the theories of fate psychoanalysis and familial depth psychology that make him an heir to Freud and Jung.

Do such bizarre occurrences actually happen in the real world?

A woman shows up who is exactly like the wife of one of your ancestors, a man who led an absolutely wretched life. You meet this woman, fall madly in love, and decide to get married, just like your forebear did. And, on top of all this, you are studying the same subject at the very same university that he attended. Pretty creepy.

What are we to make of this?

Indeed, what could it possibly mean?

I've given you the story from the standpoint of the young man. Let's examine it again from the other side, from that of the young woman. She might have looked at it in this way:

> A man shows up who is exactly likely the
> husband of one of my female ancestors. They had
> an absolutely wretched life together. This man and
> I fall madly in love and decide to get married, just
> like my forebear did.

Now, if the young woman in our story had been aware of all this, she probably would have been as shocked by the situation as the young Szondi was.

Here is a possible explanation based on reincarnation.

Two people who used to be a couple are reborn into this world. They meet again, fall in love, and decide to get married. In other words, the two people have reincarnated and are compelled to do the same thing that they did before.

Szondi looked at it another way.

He took this unusual experience and used it to develop his own theory. He speculated that *the desires of specific ancestors are repressed in the intermediate layer of the unconscious as drives and these drives determine the object choices a person makes in love, friendship, profession, sickness, and possibly even the mode of death.*

This theory marks a brilliant advance in the field, and led Szondi to conclude that the drives of his brother who died thirty years before are what caused his unusual experience.

Is this what really happened? Possibly. But I think it is important to admit the possibility of reincarnation as well.

I have quoted Szondi's theory many times in other writings as an illustration of the Buddhist concept of karma. But, as I have continued to develop my own spiritual powers, I have gradually come to believe that this theory reflects more than a simple karmic phenomenon. I am now quite certain that it directly reflects reincarnation.

In my line of work I have come across a myriad of cases that are just as strange as this story of Szondi's. My own views are based on the accumulation of these experiences. To explain my own theories, I would like to begin by offering a few of these experiences as examples.

I have taken the liberty of arranging the particulars of these cases into a narrative format.

A Case of Insane Jealousy

"Happy families are all alike. Every unhappy family is unhappy in its own way."

Thus begins Tolstoy's *Anna Karenina*.

This is a story about a family named Takayama. When they came to see me, they were about as unhappy as any family could get.

They had been married for five years.

In the beginning of their relationship they were as

happy as two people could be.

The husband's first name is Shoji. He is the second son of an old and illustrious family from the area where he grew up. After graduating from a private university in Tokyo, he returned home to take up a position in a local bank.

Shoji's dead grandfather was one of the original founders of the bank. The Takayama family was now only a shadow of its former self, but was still substantial enough, for the time being, to assure Shoji of a comfortable future.

His wife Mieko also came from a prominent family in the area. Her family had also lost a lot since the war, but the family still owned a lot of property and was of even higher social standing than the Takayamas.

Mieko also attended private university in Tokyo. She met Shoji, who was three years older than she was, at a prefecture association New Year's party. It was love at first sight. They became inseparable.

Shoji graduated from college and went home to start his career in the bank. He impatiently waited three years for Mieko to graduate so that they could get married.

They were a superbly matched couple. He was very athletic, tall and handsome. She was an evenly featured beauty who was also an athlete, having been captain of her high school volleyball team and a member of the ski team in college. She had a bright, open personality. Mieko's parents were very pleased with the match, and Shoji's father, who had lost his wife earlier, accepted Mieko without hesitation. Shoji's older brother and his wife were also very happy about the marriage.

The only exception, for some reason, was Shoji's

81-year-old grandmother. She refused to approve of the marriage and welcome Mieko into the family. Whenever anybody asked her why, she screwed up her face and refused to give any kind of real answer. Finally, her younger brother came to see her and asked her point blank what the problem was.

"Why are you being so stubborn about this?" he pressed.

"I have a really bad feeling about it. I just can't give them my blessings," she answered him begrudgingly.

"Is there something wrong with her?" he kept trying.

"No, it's nothing like that."

"Then there's nothing to talk about. You're being a selfish old woman," he countered.

His criticism silenced her. The wedding arrangements went ahead as planned.

Later on, when they were alone, the grandmother mused to Shoji's sister: "I feel like I'm suffocating whenever that girl is in the house."

Now Shoji was the second son, so he went off and established a household of his own. Mieko and his grandmother never had to live together.

One year later the grandmother died. As she lay dying, the young couple brought her the news that Mieko was pregnant but she didn't respond. She just continued to stare out into space.

Mieko had her baby. Then she began to change. She became obsessed with a completely irrational jealousy. Everyone around her began to notice. They started to wonder if she was going crazy.

Mieko started to call her husband at least once an hour

when he was at work. She was absolutely convinced that he was off having affairs with other women.

Shoji was a good man and a serious banker who treasured his wife and child. There was never even a whiff of scandal about him and other women. Mieko should have known that were totally ungrounded, but she was so delusional that as soon as he left home she became so anxious that she couldn't sit still.

Her family got together and confronted her. When they tried to reason with her she cried and apologized for her behavior, but as soon as Shoji went off to work and she was by herself again she fell under the spell of her delusions.

She had trouble doing the housework and taking care of their child.

She developed a persecution complex and became convinced her husband was going to abandon her for another woman.

The family took Mieko in for a number of psychiatric examinations. The doctor diagnosed her as mildly neurotic but not mentally disturbed.

The situation got so bad that if Shoji hadn't been connected to the bank through his grandfather he probably would have had to resign.

His relatives couldn't sit by and do nothing. They started to suggest that maybe he should divorce her. When Mieko got wind of this, she fled the house in the middle of the night with her baby in her arms. There was an all-out hunt to find her. She was finally discovered staggering along the banks of the River Oh, when she was brought back home. It only took one look to see that she wasn't pretending to be deranged. From that point on, someone had to keep an eye on her all the time. Her symptoms had escalated into severe pathology.

Shoji saw his wife being tormented by this insane jealousy and it broke his heart. He never once thought of divorcing her, but he began to fear that she would try to escape her torment through suicide. He didn't know what to do. He started to think that maybe it would be best if he killed her and the baby and then took his own life.

The Takayamas began to look for a religious or spiritual organization that could help them. They visited a few places before they came to see me. This was pretty much the state they were in when they arrived.

I immediately understood that Mieko was suffering the negative influence of a disembodied spirit.

This kind of negative influence manifests in a variety of forms. In general, these manifestations can be divided into two broad categories.

Reincarnation and Possession

These categories are possession and reincarnation.

It is very difficult to distinguish the two of these from one another.

It is not so hard, when you have the psychic ability of spiritual sight, to make the initial determination that someone is being effected by some kind of negative spiritual influence. But, no matter how psychic you are, it is very difficult to distinguish whether the cause involves reincarnation or not.

This kind of understanding requires the knowledge of special esoteric principles and techniques such as those contained in *The Six Yogas of Naropa* or those concerning the *bardo* found in *The Tibetan Book of the Dead*. The Tibetans also teach a technique known as the 'summoning of spirits'. I mastered this technique and received the title of lama from Nedon Gatsal Ling, one of the main monasteries of the Nyingma Sect. This is what empowered me with the vision to understand immediately that Mieko was suffering from the negative influence of reincarnation.

This is what I saw:

Mieko was the reincarnation of a woman who had tragically committed suicide.

The woman had fallen in love with a man from her neighborhood who promised to make her his bride and then abandoned her. The man was an ancestor of the Takayama family who had lived four generations ago. Instead of marrying the woman, he ran off with somebody else. I could see that they traveled a great distance.

Unfortunately, the deserted woman was pregnant. Devastated over being dumped and at a loss what to do about the baby, she threw herself in a river and drowned.

A few years later the man separated from the woman he had run away with and came back home. Being the second son, he went ahead and set up his own branch of the Takayama family. Apparently, he made reparations to the dead woman's family in the form of a cash payment.

I saw psychically that Mieko was the reincarnation of

the woman who committed suicide by drowning herself.

I explained these things to Mr. and Mrs. Takayama, and asked them to try to verify as many of the facts of the story as they could. Even though it happened a long time ago, I thought there might be some surviving family member who knew something about it.

"I understand what you are saying," Shoji replied. "But I have complete faith in your powers to see what you have seen. Since I'm already sure that it's the truth, isn't there anything we can start doing right away to make things better?"

I answered him:

"The first thing you need to do is to corroborate as much of the information as you can. And don't spare any effort in your search, do everything you can to find out what happened—that in itself will act to honor the dead woman. I know you might not be able to discover anything, but keep looking.

"Your wife is going to be fine. Now that we understand the root cause of her problem, she'll get better soon. You should both try to relax."

Mieko seemed completely stunned by this information. She was staring at my face.

I asked her, "Mrs. Takayama, I understand that you are quite athletic. Do you know how to swim?"

Mieko looked dumbfounded.

"How in the world do you know that? I can do just about any sport, but swimming has always been a real sore point. I can't do it at all."

As she was saying this, a look of realization and shock passed over her face.

"Is *that* the reason why?" she exclaimed.

I nodded at her and smiled.

A person who reincarnates after an unnatural death has knowledge of the circumstances of that death lodged somewhere in their deep memory. For example, someone who has been stabbed to death is usually afraid of knives. Or someone who has drowned will be afraid of water. It is no surprise that Mieko was unable to go near the water from the time she was a little girl. When she was wandering about on that riverbank carrying her child she really might have killed herself—she was very close to the end.

My knowledge about her fear of water is what convinced Mieko that I really did have the power to see into the spiritual dimension. Up until that point she wasn't totally convinced. Suddenly, the color in her face improved and her whole countenance brightened.

Finally, Shoji said, "If this is what is going on, does that mean that I am the reincarnation of the man who betrayed her?"

"No," I answered, and had to laugh. "There's no way you are the reincarnation of that heartless fellow. Don't give that a second thought."

This made both of them feel much better, and they went home.

A few days later, Shoji came back to see me by himself.

He told me he found out that his great uncle, the older brother of his dead grandmother, remembered having heard something about this woman when he was a young child.

"When he was a boy he heard stories about a man in

our family from the last generation who had done something very sinful. He hurt a young woman so badly that she drowned herself. Apparently, that branch of the family held a memorial service for her every year until the beginning of the war. But I guess this means that she still bears a grudge against us, doesn't she?"

I nodded, and asked him, "So how is your wife? Is she feeling better?"

"Thank you so much for asking. Thanks to your invaluable help, she is feeling much better. I was even able to leave her at home by herself today. She says that her anxiety is utterly gone now that she understands the reason for her problems. Before, it was like something was gripping her by the throat and she was always a nervous wreck. Yet she still feels that she won't have total peace of mind until she is sure that the soul of the dead woman has completely attained liberation. Please help us make that happen."

I nodded again and told him, "I've already given the unfortunate woman a posthumous Buddhist name and started services for the liberation of her soul, so you can rest assured that she will be fine."

"Thank you so very, very much. Please excuse my asking, but could I ask you what name you've given her?"

I wrote two names down on a piece of paper and handed it to him.

Agon'in-shakuni-jiku-Miei-shinnyo
Agon'in-shaku-shuko-Zen-dojo

"The name Zen-dojo is for the baby who the mother was carrying when she died. Apparently, the baby was a girl. (*dojo* means 'little girl'.) Her mother committed suicide in the autumn. (The *shu* in *shuko* means 'autumn'.)"

Shoji instantly became pale.

"I'm sorry, I'm just so surprised. This name comes as quite a shock."

"Why is that?"

"Because my great uncle told me that the woman's name was something like Miyo or Miya. When I heard that I was startled because the name is so much like Mieko's. And now you're telling me that you gave this name *Miei-shinnyo* to the dead woman..."

Shoji sat there shaking his head in wonderment.

This is the end of the story. *Agon'in-shakuni-jiku-Miei-shinnyo* has attained liberation. Mieko Takayama has now returned to the cheerful, open-hearted person she was before her baby was born. She says she doesn't understand how she ever became so consumed with jealousy.

The whole episode now seems like a dream.

The pain and vindictiveness that *Miei-shinnyo* felt as a result of her suicide, of having been pregnant and abandoned, was probably the cause of her rebirth. She may also, in part, have still been attached to the man who betrayed her. I believe it is these strong emotional complexes of love and hate that caused her to be reborn into this life.

However, it was never made clear to me why Mieko was reborn into the Motomura family. *Miei-shinnyo*'s family didn't live anywhere near the Motomuras, and there is no ostensible connection between the two families. And, as I told Shoji, he is not the reincarnation of the hard-hearted fellow who destroyed *Miei-shinnyo*. In fact, he doesn't seem to be the reincarnation of anyone connected to this tragedy. So we also don't know why he married *Miei-shinnyo*'s reincarnation Mieko. But one thing is clear to me. I feel sure that if the situation had continued to progress the way it was heading, it would have ended badly. The whole family could have ended up dead. Would that have resolved the pain and vindictiveness that *Miei-shinnyo* was feeling towards the Takayama family?

Or else, Mieko might have been abandoned by Shoji (like if he divorced her). In that case, she probably would have drowned herself, taking her child with her. If that had happened we could say that Mieko (as per Szondi) was repeating the fate of *Miei-shinnyo*.

I believe that the situation would have resulted in one of these eventualities.

In addition, when I was looking into Mieko's situation I discovered some unexpected information. I found out that *Miei-shinnyo* had been a man in a former life. Upon further investigation, I saw that this man lived two generations before *Miei-shinnyo* and that he had been involved in a double suicide. I didn't say anything about this to Mr. and Mrs. Takayama, but I went ahead and gave this man a posthumous Buddhist name and started services for the liberation of his soul. This was necessary to ensure that Mieko would be fully liberated from her karma.

I didn't take the investigation to the point where I figured out who this man was, but I have to assume that he was either an ancestor of the Motomura family or somehow connected to them. This would make sense in terms of Mieko's birth into the Motomura family.

Beyond Depth Psychology

This is one example where my spiritual investigation into a case reveals the involvement of reincarnation.

Let's compare what I found to Dr. Szondi's theory that *"The drives of the ancestors that are repressed within the individual function unconsciously to determine the object choices the person makes in love, friendship, profession, sickness, and possibly even the mode of death."*

It doesn't seem to apply here, because *Miei-shinnyo* is not an ancestor, a blood relation, of Mieko's. Yet nevertheless her drives were determining Mieko's behavior.

So, can Szondi's theory account for this?

There is the possibility, as I noted in the last section, that *Miei-shinnyo* may somehow be related to Mieko's family the Motomuras through her former life as the man who committed love suicide. But it is questionable if even that would make her an ancestor.

There is also the possibility that somewhere in Mieko's ancestry is a woman who had an overwhelming, unrequited jealousy towards her own husband and is still carrying that feeling around in her spiritual form. There is a slight possibility that something like that might have happened.

I don't think Szondi's theory accounts for his own experience, either. When I examine his experience from the perspective I have gained in years of using my spiritual sight to try to help troubled souls, it would seem that it is an example of reincarnation. I think that trying to account for the incident within the confines of depth psychology is somewhat unreasonable.

Here is why.

Let's briefly review Szondi's experience.

A man's older brother used to study medicine at the University of Vienna. When he was there he met a woman, fell in love, and got married. She was an ethnic Aryan from Saxony, a beautiful blonde, and a linguistics teacher.

Ten odd years after this woman died, the younger brother comes to study medicine at the University of Vienna. He meets a woman, falls in love, and wants to marry her. The second woman is just like the first one. She is an ethnic Aryan from Saxony, a beautiful blonde, and a linguistics teacher.

Is there any way that all of these facts could be coincidences?

That's a hard concept to swallow. If we take a step back, making room for conjecture, we might admit the possibility that a woman just like the first one showed up in Vienna years after the first one died. But then to conclude it's mere coincidence that she runs into this particular man, who just happens to be attending classes at the same medical school as his dead brother, and that they fall in love and decide to get married is too much of a stretch.

It doesn't seem like it could be coincidence. It just doesn't seem possible for so many coincidences to happen one right after another. Instead, I believe we must conclude that these occurrences were somehow 'inevitable'. And insofar as they were inevitable, there has to have been some kind of powerful force functioning behind them that directed them to occur.

Szondi himself seems to feel the same way:

"What in the world is going on here?"

At that moment he was deeply rocked by a powerful intuition.

This wasn't a coincidence at all.

It was a warning, some kind of sign.

In a flash, it dawns on him that something in his unconscious mind is compelling him to repeat the behavior pattern of his older brother.

He suddenly becomes terrified that he will repeat the fate of his older half-brother.

He doesn't understand where this drive to repeat his brother's fate is coming from, but he intuitively understands that it is something he must resist.

Szondi believed his experience was not coincidental.

So, if it was inevitable, what kind of power made it happen?

What kind of power made this woman appear on earth and made Szondi meet up with her?

Dr. Szondi's answer is that "the drives of the ancestors repressed within the individual" made it happen.

His brother's marriage had been a total disaster. And then some time after their wretched life together, his brother is believed to have committed suicide. Moreover, a number of years after that, the wife met such a miserable death that she might as well have committed suicide herself.

Lipot Szondi was born three years after his older

half-brother died.

What kind of desire made the older brother plant this kind of compulsion in the unconscious mind of his descendant?

Could it have been a desire to rectify his failed marriage, to make a happy life together with this woman?

Or could it have been a desire to take revenge on the woman who had entrapped him into such unhappiness?

Or could he possibly want to go through the same thing all over again?

Of course, the same holds true for the woman. Did she have the desire to manifest on earth because she wanted to rectify her marriage to Szondi's brother and manage to have a happy life this time around?

Or was she driven by the desire to vent her hostility, to get revenge on the man who caused her so much unhappiness?

Or did she simply want to repeat the fate she had experienced in her last lifetime?

When you think about it, whatever the underlying cause of the manifestation, the individual's drives somehow cause a replica of itself to be reborn, one with the same appearance and occupation and in a similar environment as the original.

This is nothing other than reincarnation.

I need to note that in my work I do see cases which can be adequately explained by Szondi's theory.

I don't accept as true that repressed consciousness has the power to create duplicate manifestations of an individual, down to physical appearance, occupation, and all other circumstances. I don't believe that the repressed consciousness of any given individual has this kind of power.

But reincarnation does.

Depth-psychological theories cannot always account for the extent of the ancestral manifestation. I would suggest that there has to be a greater force at work here, one that does not belong to this world.

This immediately brings up another question.

Does 'reincarnation', or 'rebirth', have the kind of mysteriouse power to create duplicate manifestations?

I have to say yes.

Individuals who reincarnate do seem to have this kind of miraculous power.

I'll go on to explain this in more detail, but first let me conclude this section.

I suspect that Lipot Szondi, to a certain extent, had an idea similar to the one I've just expressed above.

Look at what he wrote in his book *Unmei e no chosen* (*Triebpalhologie*, translated by Ryuzo Satake, Kanazawa Bunko.)

Szondi selected the name for his own brand of research (fate analysis) for the following reasons.

Szondi takes not only the mind but also the body, not only the drives and hereditary characteristics but also the function of the soul, as the central focus of his depth-psychological research. He treats these phenomena as not only belonging to this present existence but to future existences as well. The word 'fate' serves to conceptually unify body and soul, and therefore to integrate individual and interpersonal phenomena of this existence with those of future ones. In this way, his approach towards depth psychology became that of 'fate science' (*Schicksalswissenschaft*). He called his own approach 'the dialectic investigation of fate' (*dialektische Anankologie*).

With the passage of time fate analysis has developed into a whole new branch of inquiry complete with its own methods of psychological diagnosis and treatment. No matter how far we take this, however, fate analysis will always remain within the boundaries of depth psychology for the very reason that it takes as its object of study the important territory of the unconscious known as the familial unconscious. And the familial unconscious regulates the specific area of human existence known as 'selective fate', the selective function which controls individual fate and, by extension, interpersonal and communal fate as well.

In this passage, Lipot Szondi uses the words 'function of the soul'. Furthermore, he says, "he treats these (central) phenomena as not only belonging to this present existence but to future existences as well."

The use of the term present and future existences implies a belief in past existence as well.

I do believe that the notions of rebirth and reincarnation were within Szondi's intellectual purview. However, I believe that if he had raised them for consideration it would have taken the discourse outside the framework of the 'science' of psychology. I believe this is why he makes the comment that it (fate analysis) "will always remain within the boundaries of depth psychology."

Depending on one's ideology, Szondi's fate analysis could be considered a psychological inquiry into the subject of reincarnation.

And finally...

I'm still concerned about what happened to the woman who Lieutenant Szondi left behind.

Lieutenant Szondi definitely took a wise course of action. For a young man, he acted in an exceptionally rational manner. It's not surprising that he later became a world-renowned scholar.

But whatever happened to her?

I have the feeling she probably didn't deal with the situation as well as he did. It's never easy for anyone to deal with rejection, but when we think about this woman's former lifetime, it must have been very difficult for her. If she was someone who was able to resolve emotional conflict, she never would have reincarnated in this way in the first place.

I imagine that Lieutenant Szondi returned to his regiment without ever speaking to her again.

You can't talk your way out of a mess like this. It's hard to say goodbye to someone and walk away. She would have made a scene. There would have been hours of tearful recriminations.

Szondi tells us he returned to his regiment that very day, leading me to believe that he just got out of there without explaining anything to her. Under the circumstances, this was probably the smartest thing he could have done. He may have even believed that he was doing what he could to spare her further unhappiness.

But I suspect this wasn't the end of it for her.

She probably had an unhappy life that somehow mimicked her former one. I'm afraid that she may have met with a miserable death like she did before.

This woman will definitely be back again!

The Mysterious Power of the Reincarnates

In the previous section, I suggested that reincarnates have a mysterious power to replicate their former lives to a great degree.

This power enables them to duplicate many of the circumstances, conditions, and personal relationships from before.

I don't know where this power comes from. But I am certain that they have it.

Maybe it comes from the same place that engenders reincarnation itself.

Not many people seem aware of this odd power, but when examining reincarnates the nature of its importance becomes clear.

Let me explain what I mean.

Recently, in Europe and the United States, there appears to be a rapid increase in the number of people who believe in reincarnation.

There have always been a significant number of people

who held this belief, but few were comfortable writing or speaking about it openly. This is because reincarnation was not recognized by Christian doctrine. The recent change in the prevailing atmosphere is largely due to two reasons.

The first of these is the psychic counseling work done by the clairvoyant Edgar Cayce.

Cayce used his clairvoyance to divine the past lives of his clients. He used the resulting information to guide his clients toward resolution of a variety of problems.

Cayce referred to these clairvoyant sessions as 'readings', and performed over 18,000 of them during his lifetime. He may have made the occasional error, but his clairvoyance proved accurate in a majority of cases.

Edgar Cayce became famous for his readings, and as his fame spread, more and more people began to accept the idea that reincarnation is real.

The second factor leading to the increased acceptance of reincarnation is connected to the aftermath of the Holocaust that the Nazis perpetrated on the Jewish people.

The Jewish Holocaust began with the Nazi invasion of Poland in September 1939. The Nazis ultimately exterminated 6,000,000 Jewish people.

Some of the people in this large group have been reincarnating, one by one. They have started to go public with memories of their past lives. And because so many people were killed, record numbers are reincarnating. Large numbers of people may have been killed in other historical periods, but nothing like what happened during the Holocaust. And people from other destructive times have tended to reincarnate over a longer period of time, so it has not been as easy to verify their claims of rebirth.

The facts of the Jewish Holocaust, however, are still fresh in our minds. This makes it possible to investigate the memories the reincarnates claim to have.

In fact, much investigative work is being done on the past life memories of people who believe that they died in the Holocaust by both scientists and journalists. This work has found corroborative evidence in a large percentage of cases. Such information has been released to the general public, and has furthered the increasing acceptance of the notion of reincarnation as something that is true.

The extermination of the Jews was an unspeakable atrocity, but the very horror of it creates extremely vivid past life memories in those that have them.

We now have recorded cases of people who were not born in Germany, have never been there, and who don't have any direct knowledge of the concentration camps but who, nevertheless, remember the camps so clearly that they can draw maps pinpointing the locations of specific buildings in the camps where they were interned. The facts have been investigated and the memories proved correct.

Rabbi Yonassan Gershom writes about one such reincarnate whose name is Judy. The following is excerpted from his book *Beyond the Ashes*:

> Judy (is) an American exchange student who spent her junior year of high school in Germany. While there, she went on a tour which included a visit to the former site of the Dachau concentration camp. As a sickening familiarity stirred within her, it was, she said, like being in two lives at the same time. Everything was frighteningly familiar,

and she knew where all of the buildings had stood and what they were used for, even before the guide explained it. The building where she had died was long since torn down, but she knew exactly where it had been, and on the screen of her memory she say her own death.

Throughout the tour, Judy kept having the sensation of walking in mud, although the weather was very dry and the path was graveled. (In fact, during the 1940s there had been no gravel, only endless mud.) Later, when she removed her shoes, the soles were dry, but somehow her feet and socks had gotten muddy. Was it perspiration? Or had she somehow "walked" into another life?[i]

Somehow "walked" into another life? Nothing of the sort. She hadn't visited her previous life. And the moisture, of course, was not perspiration.

Judy was a reincarnate who had the ability to replicate certain conditions of her former existence. I sincerely doubt that she was aware of it, but she was someone who was endowed with the power to manifest certain situations and conditions of an earlier time.

We need to factor this into any discussion of reincarnation.

Rabbi Gershom relates another, similar, example:

Beverly was a single mother in her thirties, whom I first met through a social service agency in

---

i. Rabbi Yonasson Gershom, *Beyond the Ashes*, pp. 30–31

1984. Her father was non-Jewish, her mother Jewish, but very secretive about it. In fact, Beverly's parents did not even tell her that she was Jewish until adulthood. Therefore, she (had no) training in Jewish customs, teachings, or beliefs...

But now that Beverly had found out about her background, she was eager to explore her heritage. She was a deeply spiritual person and had felt frustrated that her parents had never really practiced any religion. Nor had Beverly been able to study on her own, because she was functionally illiterate. This is important information, because not only had she never read the Bible, she also had not read books on psychic phenomena or the Holocaust.

Over the next few months, Beverly and I became friends, and she often came to our house for the Sabbath or Jewish holidays. One such Sabbath afternoon, after we had finished the traditional meal and were sharing personal stories, the subject turned to dreams. Cautiously at first, as if she were afraid that I might not believe her, Beverly told my wife Caryl and me about a recurring childhood nightmare.

In the dream she was a little boy about seven or eight years old, standing in a line with his mother. Beverly described how they got to a table where a man was telling some people to go to the left and others to the right. He pointed and they went through a door.

The scene shifted, and they were suddenly in

a horrible place, where there was a terrible smell. Some men were throwing people into a fire alive, and then the little boy was thrown in, too. He kept patting himself trying to put out the flames, then he died.

At this point in Beverly's narrative, I suddenly began to smell burning flesh. Excusing myself from the table, I went to the kitchen, even though we are vegetarians and it was not logical to be looking for meat in our oven. Still, it was the natural place to check for something burning.

Everything was fine in the kitchen. But I could still smell smoke, so I decided to look outside. No sooner had I walked out the door onto the front porch, than the smell was gone! None of my neighbors were barbecuing, nor was there any other kind of fire that could account for what I had smelled.[ii]

The Rabbi goes on to cite more evidence of Beverly's reincarnation. In my own work, I have encountered a number of cases that are as vivid as this.

This kind of incarnate being has the power to actually reconstruct attributes of their former existences—the fate, circumstances, and personal relationships that characterized the past life.

This is not a 'repetition' of fate. It is more correctly a 'reappearance'.

Almost all reincarnates have the power to do this to a

---

ii. Gershom, op. cit., pp. 20-22

greater or lesser degree, though the degree of the power varies greatly from individual to individual.

This kind of reincarnation soon becomes problematic. The reincarnate, in a sense, deserves what they get because of their negative karma. But the people they are in relationship with are bound to suffer as well. Mieko's husband is a perfect example.

Because Mieko's husband is not this sort of negatively driven reincarnate, it is not clear what kind of karma binds them together as man and wife. All we know for certain is that he is the second son of the Takayama family. It's hard to understand how this would be enough to get him into the difficult situation he finds himself in as Mieko's husband.

And yet, this same sort of inexplicably tragic, miserable, and unfortunate situation happens all the time in this world.

Here is another disturbing example.

"Was Killing Him the Only Solution?"

One morning, Hisae was busily serving breakfast while her husband Yoshizo sat at the table sipping his tea and reading the newspaper. He picked up the section he was reading and held it out to her, silently indicating with his eyes that she should take a look at one of the articles. She looked back at him questioningly, and he again motioned to the article in the paper that he wanted her to read.

She took one glance at the headline and her expression froze. The print leapt up at her from the page:

MURDER TRIAL OPENS OF HIGH SCHOOL TEACHER ACCUSED OF KILLING SON IN DOMESTIC DISPUTE— DEFENSE CLAIMS MITIGATING CIRCUMSTANCES

Holding her breath, Hisae began to read:

Opening arguments began on the 7th in the murder trial of former high school teacher Makoto Saito (54) and his wife Tsuyumi (49) of Ryoke 1-chome, Urawa City. The defendants are accused of stabbing their eldest son to death in response to domestic violence. The case is being tried in District First Criminal Court, Judge Mikio Hibi presiding.

In the arraignment, the prosecution was granted a full indictment against both of the defendants.

According to the indictment, Mr. Saito killed his eldest son Jun (23) on the morning of June 4th while his son was asleep. The victim died from stab wounds to his abdomen and chest made by a kitchen or butcher knife. Mrs. Saito is named as his accomplice, and is accused of bashing in her son's head with a toy gun and of handing her husband the knife.

In opening arguments, the prosecuting attorney stated that the murder victim had dropped out of college in March of 1990. The victim then took a part-time job, and tried to establish a career as a musician. His lifestyle deteriorated. He became an alcoholic, and began sleeping all day and partying all night. Episodes of violent behavior began in the summer of 1991. He started destroying domestic property and abusing his parents.

Defense quoted Makoto as saying, "We were very worried about how this might affect our two younger sons..."

Makoto talked about retiring and moving away with his wife and youngest son so that Jun could have the house to himself. But Jun's violent behavior continued.

The grandfather, who was living with them at the time, died. The family interred his ashes in late May. That same night, Jun had another violent outburst. His parents looked at him and thought, "We gave birth to him and now we've got to deal with this." They decided to kill him.

Tsuyumi claimed she was "grasping at straws". She went for domestic abuse counseling to a religious group in Omiya City, and then tried to convince Jun to go there to pray.

Defense counsel posed the question, "Could any of us have found an ideal solution to this intolerable situation?" He then went on to detail the particulars of the violence that had pushed the family to its absolute limits. He built an argument to support his claim of extenuating circumstances.

The question "Was killing him the only solution?" was raised in tandem by the defense, the prosecution, and the judge. In response, Makoto let out a deep sigh and confessed: "If you only knew what he was like. He refused to get help. Every time we tried to reason with him, he just got worse and we became more desperate. To this day I really don't know what else we could have done."

Makoto pleaded clemency for his wife, asking that she be allowed to continue raising their youngest son. He asked to take her punishment on himself.

Hisae first read about this case a few months ago. She felt great sympathy for the defendants.

Her own family, the Tsukadas, was suffering from a similar problem. Their 22-year-old son Koji had also gotten violently abusive in the last year or two. When something happened he didn't like he would explode like a crazy person and start screaming and trashing whatever household objects he could get his hands on. It didn't matter how valuable anything was. Once he got started on a rampage he was unstoppable.

When she first read about the murder in the paper, she felt sorry for everyone involved but still believed that her family would be able to solve their problems without violence. She could never, ever, bring herself to kill her own child.

But now the situation in her own home was so intolerable that she wasn't so sure.

She and her husband had never put it into words, but they had looked silently at each other many times and they each knew what the other was thinking: "This is bound to end up in bloodshed."

"Look at this," Yoshizo spit out through clenched teeth as he handed her another section of the paper. "It sounds just like us."

Hisae kept reading.

EVIDENCE PRESENTED AT TRIAL

The results of the investigation into the history of the victim's violent behavior were presented to the court.

Apparently, Jun was a good student and an all-around athlete in elementary and junior high school.

In the spring of 1984 he entered Saitama Prefectural Urawa High School, where he began to change. His began to fail in his studies and to isolate himself from his classmates. By the end of the first year, he quit participating in all extracurricular activities.

He became a compulsive songwriter, composing lyrics and music. By the third term of sophomore year he stopped going to school. In the spring of 1986 he quit altogether.

While working at a part-time job, Jun suddenly decided he wanted to go to college. He managed to pass the high school equivalency examination and entered Rikkyo University in

April 1987. But once there he became totally involved with a ski club and stopped going to classes. He ended up dropping out in March 1990.

He shut himself up in his room and started drinking heavily, sleeping all day and staying awake all night.

In the summer of 1991 he confessed to his parents that he was having sexual problems with the woman he was seeing. He blamed them for everything. When drunk, he'd scream, "It's all your fault that I was born like this," and then start trashing the furniture. His father's attempts to get him to see a doctor just fueled his rage. He continued to destroy things, though he wasn't beating his parents.

But the verbal abuse got worse. "I'm going to make sure you never get out of here to escape to Shikoku. I'll eat up your entire pension. I'm going to make your life hell from now on until you die. I'll make sure you get nothing but the bare necessities—then I'm going use the rest of your money to have a good time."

On the morning of June 4, 1992, the day the crime was committed, Jun had been drinking heavily. He again accused his parents of causing his problems, and told them they had to buy him an apartment. They decided they were going to have to kill him to protect the rest of the family. They murdered him together that afternoon.

Hisae read through the article a number of times, then

silently looked at the face of her husband.

"See, it's just the same," he was muttering to himself over and over.

Hisae knew what he meant.

Especially the part where the victim was quoted as saying:

> "I'll eat up your entire pension. I'm going to make your life hell from now on until you die. I'll make sure you get nothing but the bare necessities —then I'm going to use the rest of your money to have a good time."

Koji had thrown the same threat in their faces.

The only thing different was that the money he was trying to extort from them wasn't her husband's pension. Instead, he wanted them to sell all the land and rental property they had inherited and turn the money over to him.

Not that they owned that much property any longer. There had been quite a bit up until the war, but post-war agricultural reform, among other things, had reduced their family holdings to little more than three or four small parcels of land. Koji wanted them to sell everything that was left. They had already been forced to sell off two pieces of property to pay for a sports car and credit card purchases that he bought.

"I'm going to make your life hell from now on until you die." He had even used the exact same line as the murder victim. How could any child born from their own blood say such a thing? They didn't have a clue how things could have turned out this way.

When Koji said this kind of awful thing to them, it was like he was a cauldron of seething hatred. His whole countenance changed, as he spit out his venom over and over again from between clenched teeth. It was horrifying, as if he had suddenly become somebody else, a total stranger.

The words "How did we ever give birth to such a child?" escaped helplessly from Hisae's mouth for the umpteenth time.

The victim in the murder case had never actually attacked his parents, but this was not the case with Koji. He had never raised his hand to his father, but he had severely bruised his mother any number of times, nearly breaking bones in her arms and legs.

The worst thing was when he brandished a knife. He'd never done more than threaten them with it, but that was enough to terrify them completely.

Just three months ago Koji had stuck a jack-knife into the pillar of the entryway of their house. The Takadas were made so despondent and powerless by his continual intimidation that they agreed to sell another piece of land at a big loss.

Their fear that this situation was going to end in bloodshed was becoming more and more likely.

How had this ever happened?

No matter how much they tried, they couldn't figure out what was making Koji behave like this.

And the abuse continued. Whenever Koji opened his mouth it was to throw more accusations at them. Now he was saying, "It's your fault that I'm so stupid. This whole thing is your responsibility." This started right after he failed his college entrance exam for the second time. Up until that point he'd had a dark side, but he definitely hadn't been a violent person. On the contrary, he'd been a rather shy, reflective, passive, soft-spoken kind of kid.

When he was very young he hadn't spoken much at all, maybe because he had a tendency to stutter when he got a bit excited. But he definitely wasn't stupid. He had been in the upper percentiles of his class during junior and senior high.

The Tsukadas had three children. Koji had gotten along well with his siblings.

The Inferno

Yoshizo Tsukada was born into a good family of N City near Nagoya. After graduating from college, he took a job with a local ceramics concern. With two years left to go until he reached retirement age, Yoshizo was now 58 and head of the sales division. His upright nature made him naturally well-suited to a conservative industry like that of his company. He was well liked by his regular clients, and there was talk that he was going to be promoted to the position of director before long.

His eldest son Ryota had graduated from a college in Tokyo two years ago, and stayed there to take a job with a trading firm. He was still single.

His daughter Yayoi had graduated from high school last year and gotten into a junior college. She was now living at his younger brother's house and going to school.

Both Ryota and Yayoi were excellent students. However, as noted, Koji was not stupid. But whereas both of the other children had gotten into their first-choice schools, Koji had struggled. Failing the entrance exam for the second time left him badly shattered. He shut himself up in his room on the second floor, and practically stopped going to cram school. He blared his stereo or television every night until dawn. Then he'd go to sleep and sleep all day. When he got up, he'd eat the food that Hisae had prepared for him and then aimlessly head out downtown. He'd come home drunk late at night and go upstairs to his room without saying a word to anybody. The only time he talked to them was to demand money.

Whenever Koji was in the house, Hisae was so nervous she jumped at the slightest sound; when he was out, she worried constantly about what kind of trouble he was getting himself into. She was always anxious and unable to get any rest.

Both Hisae and Yoshizo were glad that Ryota was off working in Tokyo. Koji had started to become violent right around the time that his older brother had left the house, and they feared what might have happened if Ryota had decided to take a job closer to home. There was always the chance that Ryota, who was three years older than Koji, might have been able to exert some control over his younger brother's behavior. But then when they saw what Koji was like when he was in one of his insane rages, they decided it was probably better that Ryota wasn't there.

Koji had never been rough with Yayoi, but she was still very afraid of him so, on the pretense that it was closer to school, they had arranged for her to stay with her uncle.

A month later Koji did something that made them believe they were really in trouble. They went blind with fear, and thought the end might be near.

Koji fell in love with a woman and announced that they were going to open a bar before they got married. Koji demanded that his parents fork over the capital to start the new business.

He needed a sum in the 5 figures, and started to hound them mercilessly for it. There was no way they could come up with that amount. He insisted that they sell more property, but land wasn't something that you could sell so easily. Plus, they had the future wedding plans of their other two children to think about.

"Just think about what you're asking. It's completely impossible..." Hisae cried as she tried to pacify her son. But he wouldn't listen. Instead, he knocked her to the ground and whipped out a knife. It didn't seem like he was really going to hurt her, but Yoshizo couldn't stand by and do nothing so he tried to get his son to stop. Koji kicked him in the stomach and threw him down on the ground.

"Had enough? You'd better come up with the money by the end of the month or next time I won't let you off so easy," he yelled as he threw a few things against the wall before he ran off down the street.

That night the two of them went to stay with

Yoshizo's younger brother, where Yayoi was living.

Hisae admitted that she was too scared of her own son to stay in her own house. Yoshizo decided it was time to talk over the situation with his younger brother and his brother's wife.

Hisae and Yoshizo had told the other couple a little bit about Koji's violent behavior, but it was such a private matter that they hadn't gone into a lot of detail. Now when Yoshizo described what was really going on, the other couple was absolutely shocked. They had no idea what to do either.

The next morning Koji called. His uncle answered the phone. "If you guys can afford to shelter my family, then you can afford to give me the money I need," Koji yelled at him. There was no way to reason with him.

"Maybe we should just move out of there and let him keep the house," Hisae said tearfully. "Maybe that's the only way we can be over and done with all of this." There was nothing anyone could say to her.

A friend of Yoshizo's brother and his wife's suggested that the Tsukadas come to see me. They were still in the middle of this horrible situation.

The Mystery of the Birthmark

Spiritual interference.

I got it right away, when Mr. and Mrs. Tsukada were first telling me their story.

But just to be sure, I excused myself and went into another room to check it out. I entered a state of meditative absorption, and confirmed that, yes, that is what was happening.

This was definitely a case of spiritual interference.

I went back into the reception room and sat down in front of them.

"Mrs. Tsukada, may I ask you a question?"

"Of course," she answered as she looked at me with a tense expression on her face.

"Does Koji have any birthmarks on his body?"

"Why yes, he does."

Hisae stared at me open-mouthed as she continued. "He has two of them. One is a little below his left nipple and the other one is on the right side of his navel."

"I thought he might."

"Yes, in fact, when Koji was a little boy we used to say it was a good thing that Koji wasn't a girl. The marks are not that pronounced, but there are two bluish smudges which are each about two centimeters in diameter."

"I'm not surprised," I said. "And one more thing. When Koji was a child did he ever suddenly wake up crying and frightened in the middle of the night from nightmares?"

"Yes, he did!" Hisae exclaimed, again clearly taken aback.

"He used to have terrible nightmares once or twice a month until he went to elementary school. He'd start screaming and try to run out of the house. We were so worried about it that we went to speak to a psychiatrist at the university hospital. The doctor told us that Koji was suffering from something called 'night terrors' and that he would grow out of it naturally as he got older. He told us not to medicate him and keep him calm and relaxed. The nightmares almost stopped after he started going to junior high, and I'd completely forgotten about it until now. What does that have to do with...?"

She looked very concerned.

Before answering her, I turned to her husband Yoshizo.

"And now let me ask you something."

"Of course."

"Did you ever hear about anyone in your family who was sent overseas during the war?"

"Why yes," he answered, "there were two or three people."

"Anyone who went to China?"

"Yes, my uncle, my father's older brother, was sent to the Chinese front," he responded to the unusual line of questioning, wide-eyed with bafflement.

"The next question I have is a difficult one to ask," I said, looking directly at him. "Did you ever hear anything about your uncle killing anybody during the war?"

Yoshizo was silent for a second, then he answered in a subdued voice, "...Yes, I did. I heard something like that from my father."

I nodded and said, "Let me get straight to the point. Koji is the reincarnation of the man that your uncle killed during the war, who seems to have been a soldier in the Chinese army."

"You're kidding!" the Tsukadas reacted in unison to

this totally unexpected bit of information. They were both looking at me intently.

"I know that this must be very difficult for you to believe, but, trust me, it's the truth. I think that your uncle probably killed this Chinese soldier when they were involved in hand-to-hand combat. In any event, your uncle either stabbed or shot him to death. The birthmarks on Koji's body are like scars from those wounds. This phenomenon is something we often see in people who have been reincarnated.

"Furthermore, the night terrors Koji suffered from as a child, his screaming in the middle of the night, were caused by the past life memories. He was terrified by his dreams of being attacked. He was reliving the last few moments of the battle in which he died."

Mr. and Mrs. Tsukada exchanged glances. They sat there dumbfounded.

"When you go home, please ask the other members of your family if anyone knows more details about this story."

"Actually," said Yoshizo, "after his posting on the continent, my uncle was sent to the southern theater, where he was killed in action in the Philippines. He was the eldest son of his generation but he was still single so my father inherited the role of head of the family. So all we know is what my uncle told my father..."

And here is the summary of what Yoshizo told me:

Yoshizo's uncle was working in intelligence, assigned to duty in a counter-espionage unit. It's possible he was a member of the military police or the secret service.

His unit discovered evidence of a leak in vital information concerning certain operations, and was put on special guard. Their vigilance netted two or three Chinese suspects. Yoshizo's uncle, Sergeant T, was assigned to watch one of them very carefully. The suspect was a 22-or 23-year-old who was performing coolie labor for the outfit. He was a slow-moving guy who hardly spoke any Japanese. He always had this dumb grin on his face, and he seemed pretty dim-witted. Sargent T didn't really think it could be him, but he was keeping close tabs on the fellow just in case.

One night he got wind that the coolie was sneaking out the back gate of the compound and proceeded to follow him.

At first, the coolie walked in the same ambling way he always did. Then, all of a sudden, he quickened his pace.

Sergeant T intuitively knew that the Chinese man was about to disappear into the recesses of a nearby village and, while still behind him, yelled at him to halt. At that, the coolie took off in a run.

Sergeant T stayed right on his heels until they reached a point just this side of the hamlet. The coolie realized he was about to be caught, and without warning, turned around, unsheathed a dagger, and came after the Sergeant. The military man was carrying a revolver, but in the suddenness of the action didn't have enough time to get to it. It was all he could do to fend off the attack of the other man.

Sergeant T could tell from the look of absolute fury on the 'coolie's' face and by the disciplined movements of his body that the 'dumb' routine was all an act. Now, the Sergeant was known in his outfit as something of an expert in the martial arts, but his opponent was clearly trained as well. He unleashed such a volley of thrusts, parries, and kicks that Sergeant T couldn't find an opportunity to counterattack. Finally, the Sergeant tripped over the root of a tree and landed on the ground. Just as he was thinking it was all over, his hand fumbled upon a rock. He seized it and pounced on his attacker with all his might, going for the guy's face. He managed to connect, and his enemy let out a blood-curdling yell as he was thrown off balance.

Sergeant T was finally able to draw his gun and fire. That's when he noticed that he was seriously wounded in his right arm and shoulder.

Yoshizo quoted what his uncle had declared pensively to his father:

"I was sure I was a goner there for a while. We found out later that this Chinese operative, even though he was young, was a very important spy. It turns out he spoke fluent Japanese. These Chinese are really something."

The result of my consultation with the Tsukadas was that I advised them not to breathe a word about any of this to Koji. Hisae kept insisting that it felt too weird to live in the same house with him, knowing what she did now. I tried to reason with her.

"But you are his parents. There isn't anything you can do to escape that fact. You are going to have to get over any misgivings that you may be feeling.

"Just think about this for a minute. If we look back only 5 generations we find over 100 ancestors. If we go back 7 or 8 generations, this explodes into an enormous number. Among all these possibilities, there are bound to be some individuals who are connected to people with whom they have a fundamentally adversarial relationship.

They might even end up married to someone like that. Similarly, there have to be a lot of people who have come into our family tree from other countries. This means that there is foreign blood in all of our veins. So you need to understand that this sort of situation isn't really that strange or unusual. It's just that most of the time we aren't aware of all these different factors.

"Believe me, I've seen this kind of thing many, many times. And I don't always tell the clients everything I see. Often I just remain quiet about most of it, and go ahead and try to take care of the situation by doing things like conducting services of liberation for the troubled souls I encounter in our consultation sessions. In cases where I think that giving the clients a lot of information will have negative repercussions and lasting aftereffects, I may choose not to give them any information at all. But I made the determination that it was okay to tell the two of you everything. No, actually, I thought it was better if I told you everything, so I did. Mrs. Tsukada, now that we have uncovered the truth, the situation will be resolved in no time. Try to forget about it. Please just do as I tell you."

I went ahead and conferred a posthumous Buddhist name on the young Chinese soldier who had been killed in the war, and properly conducted a memorial service for the liberation of his spirit.

Three months later the atmosphere in the Tsukada household underwent a complete change. Koji decided that he was going to take the college entrance exam again. He was back at cram school everyday preparing for the tests.

His violent behavior is now a thing of the past and

seems like it never happened.

And like it never happened, I believe that in a year or two the birthmarks that Koji has on his body will fade away and disappear. I hope that, by that time, everything I told Mr. and Mrs. Tsukada will have come to seem like a very distant memory.

Again, this sort of thing is not that unusual. I've seen similar instances many times. This is not an exaggeration. I've encountered it over and over. Here are a few more examples.

Various Examples of Reincarnation

Here is one from a consultation letter that I just happen to have right in front of me.

Koichi Takeyama
K City
Age 63

I am suffering from domestic violence at the hands of my eldest son, Hideo Takeyama. My body is battered all over from where he has punched me. He kicks me when he's wearing leather shoes. I am in a great deal of pain. I have a hemorrhage in my right eye, both my legs and my left arm are bruised and swollen, and blows to my chest have made it hurt when I breathe. Now he's threatening to douse our house with gasoline and torch it.

To top it all off, Hideo is in the middle of an ugly divorce suit. He has threatened to kill my wife and me if he loses.

Please help us. We beg of you.

Kyoko Takeyama
K City
Age 57

Blaming his misery on the bad upbringing he says he got from us, Hideo is always demanding that we give him money. When he doesn't like the way I respond to one of his requests, he forces me to lie down on the ground and steps on my head with his shoes on. He hits me. One time he thrust a knife into my hands and told me to slit my throat. It's a living hell.

Please help us get out of this terrible situation.

It's hard for most of us to even imagine what these people are going through. But it's actually happening. I haven't changed one word of their letter. It stands as I received it. They really must be in a living hell.

Upon investigation, I discovered that their case is also a result of the effects of negative spiritual interference, just like that of the Tsukada family described above.

I was able to perceive that the Takeyama's eldest

brother, Hideo, is also the reincarnation of a Chinese soldier who was killed during the war. But there is one major difference between the two families. A distant relative of the Takeyamas has been to China, but no one ever went to war there. It follows that no one from the family ever killed a Chinese soldier. Yet I am absolutely sure from what I saw clairvoyantly that Hideo is the reincarnation of a Chinese soldier killed during the war.

So what is the karmic reason that this soul was born into the Takeyama family? I don't know, because my spiritual investigation of the situation has not yet turned up that information.

You might find it odd that people reincarnate across national boundaries. But is important to understand that this is a common occurrence.

Let's take a look at one more example.

The names in these examples are pseudonyms.

Home to Manila

Atsuko Fujio
C City
Age 46

I have a daughter named Masami who is a sophomore in high school.

Last year, all of a sudden, she lost her desire to do anything. She had never missed school, but now she stopped going. And since the time she was five years old she was crazy about the piano, but now she suddenly stopped playing.

For no reason that we could discern, she started saying that she wanted to die. She tried to slit her wrists with a razor. She tried to jump off the roof of our apartment building.

The next minute she'd turn around and start acting like her old self again. Like starting to play the piano. She'd be fine for a few days, and then, without warning, she'd revert to her listless, vacant state. Then, just as suddenly as she'd stopped, she'd get out her texts and notebooks and start studying late into the night. This would go on for a couple of days and then she'd slip back into vacuousness. She'd start saying she wished she was dead. She keeps repeating this pattern.

We finally forced her to go to a psychiatrist who examined her and told us that there was nothing wrong with her.

I've been keeping a constant watch over her, but I'm having such a hard time because she's obviously in so much pain. It's like she's locked into some kind of intense battle with something.

I have to think that all this has to be due to some kind of negative spiritual interference. Please help her in any way that you can.

I met with Masami's mother and spoke to her directly.

"I looked into this matter clairvoyantly and it is clear that Masami is suffering from negative spiritual interference which is due to reincarnation."

"Reincarnation?"

"Yes. Rebirth."

Masami's mother was speechless. Even though she had surmised correctly, as she wrote in her letter, that her daughter's problems were being caused by spiritual interference, it was clear that the idea of reincarnation was never something that had entered her mind. She looked clearly surprised as she went on to ask, "What...What do you mean by that?"

"Masami is the reincarnation of somebody else. And that is why she is being affected by these negative forces.

"Another way to explain it is to say that there are certain characteristics related to Masami's former personality, habits, intelligence, and experience that are embedded in her unconscious from which she is trying to free herself. Sometimes reincarnates experience the same life and fate that they did before. When a reincarnate tries to oppose the predetermined tendencies that they bring with them from their former existence, a battle ensues which can make them appear, from the outside at least, totally incoherent and incapable of making sound judgements. What is going on with your daughter is typical of this scenario."

Masami's mother was so dumbfounded that she couldn't say anything at all for a few moments.

Finally she asked, "Are you telling me that Masami is not Masami?"

I laughed. Not because it was funny, but to try and

make her feel more at ease.

"No, that's not what I'm saying. Masami is still Masami."

"But you just said that Masami is the reincarnation of somebody else. This sounds to me like maybe she is really that other person, not my Masami."

"I understand that this must sound very strange to you. It's difficult for me to explain it clearly, but I can tell you for sure that it's common. Though most people who are being affected by this sort of thing are not aware of what is going on. I know many cases that are as strange as this one."

I tried to explain in a way that would calm her anxiety.

"There is a world-famous academic researcher into the field of reincarnation named Ian Stevenson. Among the many cases that he has documented, there is one in which a woman's dead fiancé was reborn as her son after she married somebody else.

"The woman's name is Katherine Wright. She was engaged to be married when her fiancé was killed in a car accident. One year later she married someone else. The first child they bore was a little girl, and the second was a boy. Around the time the boy became three years old, he started regaling them with memories that sounded like they might come from his mother's former fiancé. Indeed, he started to tell them about events that they knew for a fact had happened to the boyfriend. And he started to tell them things that no three-year-old child could possibly know. He shocked those around him with intimate details about people and events in the dead man's life, including the accident.

"He said things to them like, 'I was riding in a car with my friends when we veered off onto the shoulder of the road and rolled over. The door opened and I was thrown out of the car. I broke my neck and died.'

"The small boy also told them how his corpse was carried over a bridge, and how he had been at a dance right before the accident, and the name of the town where the dance had been held. Stevenson reports that when these statements were checked out, they all proved to be true, leaving no doubt in anyone's mind that this child was the reincarnation of his mother's dead fiancé.

"I imagine that the people involved in this incident also had a hard time accepting what was going on."

"Boy, some really strange things go on in this world, don't they?" she asked. "What finally happened to the family?"

"Stevenson's account doesn't go into detail about what happened after that. I imagine that they are still living it out."

Mrs. Fujio thought hard for a minute.

"So, what am I supposed to do now? Can Masami ever become her old self again?"

"Yes. I assure you that she is going to be fine. Masami will definitely become herself again."

"What can I do to help her?"

"The first thing we need to find out is who Masami is a reincarnation of and why that person happened to reincarnate as your daughter. It's crucial to pinpoint this information."

"How can we go about doing that?"

"Let's start right now. I get the impression that the

woman who Masami is a reincarnation of was not Japanese."

"Wasn't Japanese?"

"That's correct. I think she was Southeast Asian."

"A Southeast Asian woman?"

"Yes. I get the feeling that we should try to pursue this line of investigation."

To be honest, I had already understood a lot more about this situation than I was letting on, but I needed to bring Mrs. Fujio along slowly. It's important not to scare people off with too much direct information. People need time and space to build trust and confidence in the process. I have found that it is best to let the client discover his or her own answers, one question at a time.

"Now, in this regard, let me ask you something. When Masami was a little girl, was there anything that set her apart from her siblings? Tell me anything at all that you might remember."

Mrs. Fujio sat thinking about this for a bit.

"You know, there is one thing that I did think was unusual. When she was about two years old she really wanted some crayons so I got them for her. She started drawing realistic pictures of palm trees. Ocean waves and trees that looked like palm trees. I remember discussing it a number of times with my husband, because we couldn't figure out where she had ever seen a tree like that. We figured maybe she had seen it on television or something. But it was odd because we had lots of trees in our own garden, some of them the flowering kind. But instead of drawing these she drew palm trees.

"This went on even after she got to junior high school.

Of course, she drew pictures of other things as well, but her favorite subject continued to be palm trees and the ocean. And it was always the same scene, with a small island off in the distance."

I nodded. This was just like the scene that I had seen clairvoyantly. Mrs. Fujio continued.

"There's one more thing. When Masami was five she asked if she could learn to play the piano. We got her a teacher and within a month she was able to play her etudes really well. Within six moths she could play a fair rendition of a Chopin waltz. Her teacher was very surprised at this, and told me that she thought Masami was truly gifted. Masami herself was saying that she wanted to become a professional pianist, so we found her a teacher from the national conservatory. And now it's all come to this...," Mrs. Fujio said sadly, lowering her head. I nodded in sympathy.

"Don't worry. It's going to be all right. Masami is going to get better. But, now, let me ask you, last year, when Masami's behavior suddenly changed, did anything happen that seemed to precipitate the turn of events?"

Realization dawned on her face.

"Last year Masami went to Manila in the Philippines. She changed after that. That's right. She started acting strange a little while after she came back from the Philippines."

"Did she go to Manila alone?"

"No, I went with her. She'd been saying for some time that she wanted to go there and then, last year during spring vacation, some people we know were going so we joined their tour group."

"Did anything happen when you were in Manila that you thought was strange at the time?"

"Actually, something did happen!"

She went on eagerly.

"I just remembered it just now when you asked me. We were staying in Manila, sightseeing around the city. There were a number of times when Masami made a point of saying that she felt like she had been to this or that place before. She was very insistent. It made me feel a little weird so I tried to make light of it, and remember telling her that things like that happen to me all the time too. I said something like, 'Oh, you see something in the movies or in your dreams that gets stuck in your memory and then when you run across something similar in the real world you are sure that you've experienced it before.' But, you know, she looked so serious when she was making these statements that it made me feel pretty uncomfortable."

Again I nodded.

"Psychologists call this déjà vu. It's the phenomenon of feeling that you've been someplace before. Most people have experienced it at some point in their lives. Sometimes déjà vu is just a figment of the imagination, but sometimes it reflects actual experience. If the sense of déjà vu is due to reincarnation, then when you visit someplace where you actually spent time in a former lifetime, you experience an intimate feeling of familiarity. Like maybe you've never been someplace before, but you can describe what sort of building is around the next corner, or what sort of house is on the next block.

"Because reincarnation deals with the passage of time, the surroundings may have changed somewhat but the overall picture still exists in your memory. It sounds like this is what was going on with Masami. It sounds like she had memories of her past life buried deep in her unconscious, and that these memories made her do things like draw pictures of palm trees when she was a little girl."

Mrs. Fujio let out a sigh.

I continued, "I believe I understand most of this now. I'm convinced that Masami is the reincarnation of a Filipino woman. So, the next thing I have to ask is has anyone in your family ever had any connection to the Philippines?"

"Yes, they have. My father was the branch manager of the K corporation in Manila about 20 years ago. I believe he was there for about 10 years."

"Is your father still alive and well?"

"Yes."

"Do you think you could ask your father to come see me? I'd like to speak to him about this in greater detail."

"Are you suggesting that my father has something to do with all this?"

"I can't say anything for sure until I talk to him, but maybe speaking to him will help me find the key to unlock this mystery."

Mrs. Fujio was lost in thought as she left to go home.

The Story that Mrs. Fujio's Father, Kenzo Tatsumi (72), Told Me the Following Day at the Dojo

"I believe it was the year after President Marcos declared martial law with the slogan 'Building A New Society,' so it must have been 1973. Marcos was establishing new policies across the board. Domestically, he was reorganizing the system of public safety, reforming the distribution of agricultural lands, and rooting out corruption in the bureaucracy. Internationally, he was promoting foreign trade and overseas business activity. As part of his reformation effort, he confiscated half a million firearms from the general population, which instantaneously led to greater stability in public order.

They called it martial law, but in fact the government wasn't controlled by the military, and walking around the streets didn't feel oppressive, and the Philippines was experiencing a sudden surge in tourism. Also, the Philippine economy had been given a real shot in the arm by the large sums of cash that it was receiving from Japan in the way of reparations and from other sources, and it was very active. All this activity resulted in a boon for the multinational corporations who were on the scene. We hurriedly had five young employees transferred to Manila in order to meet the increased demand.

Among these transfers was a young man named Mr. K who came to us from one of the top universities. He was 29, and had joined the company five years before. Mr. K came from a good family. He was an easy-going fellow who had played baseball in school. He was decisive when necessary, altogether the perfect model of a young executive.

Both of Mr. K's parents were still alive. His father held a government position, and his older brother was a rising star in our company who was posted at that time to our London branch.

Mr. K was the number two son in the family. He had

gotten married two years before, and had just started a family. He and his wife had a baby boy the previous year. The term 'bachelor transfer' hadn't been invented yet, but all five of these men were sent to Manila without their wives and children.

This was the time when Japan was beginning its own period of unprecedented economic growth. It was very interesting to watch the way our business was expanding overseas. The atmosphere in the office was simply buzzing. We were always on the move, hustling all the time, and a lot of business got done at night.

It's the same everywhere, but in that place and time, entertaining was a crucial part of doing business. We'd decide where to go out depending on how important the client was. Most of the best clubs, like the Wells Fargo and the El Mundo, were clustered together on Rojas Avenue which ran along the coastline. We'd book tables at our favorite clubs before going out in the evening.

Well, anyway, this is the sort of environment that we found ourselves in, so the corporation had strict prohibitions about its men fraternizing with local women in a way that could lead to complicated involvements. We had young men with us, however, and sometimes they did get into trouble. One of my duties as branch manager was to resolve these kinds of situations. The biggest headache was when one of our guys would get involved with a proper young lady. When they were mixed up with a professional, we could usually fix things with an exchange of cash. But the really problems always began when money wasn't enough to take care of the situation. That's why we had such a strong taboo against this kind of thing.

Mr. K ended up transgressing the taboo.

The woman in question was named Maria Helenes. She played the piano at one of the first class clubs we used to frequent. Maria was a girl from a good family who was training to be a classical pianist. I had met her once or twice. She was a delicate beauty with excellent manners. I could understand why K had fallen madly with her. In the beginning, she had made advances toward him and he had tried to resist because of the company policy. But once his passions were aroused he was unable to stop them from taking over.

The reason I had gone to see her was to try to get them to stop seeing each other. But as soon as I started to talk to her I could tell that it wasn't going to be that easy. She was an innocent young woman who was head over heels in love with Mr. K. We've got big trouble, I thought.

K's older brother used to work under me in the company, so I called him in London to discuss the situation. I also talked it over with the main office in Japan. Everyone agreed that the only thing we could do to be sure that he wouldn't get hurt by all this was to send him home immediately. Whatever, we knew we had to get him out of there and then, over time, I would deal with Maria the best that I could.

And so I hardened my heart and handed him his transfer orders back home. I didn't say anything at all about Maria. I just gave him the papers, silently.

I may have not spoken to him about Maria, but I imagine that K got quite an earful about her over the phone from his older brother. In any event, he accepted his orders without a word.

'The sooner the better' is all I said.

He just nodded his head.

I was relieved to know that he made a plane reservation to leave in three days' time. Then two days later I heard the shocking news. About the accident...

There is a seaside resort about 100 kilometers, or two hours by car, from Manila called Nasugbu. Heading south from there are resorts all along the shore as far as a place called Caratangan. A paved road runs along the coast.

There are scenic overlooks located along the precipitous cliffs that line the road. From here you can see Lubang Island off in the distance. This is the island where Lieutenant Onoda lived in isolation for all those years while he believed that the war was still going on.

Narrow dirt roads lead off the highway. Tourists sometimes turn off onto these to try and get a better look at Lubang. There isn't any kind of barriers on these cliffs so it's quite dangerous.

The car that K and Maria were in plunged over the cliffs.

Apparently, they had spent the night in a nearby hotel, and then driven out to the cliffs. We don't know what time the accident happened. The conjecture was that it was probably around dawn. The totaled car was discovered in the morning light. There was the corpse of a woman floating out of it.

When I heard the news, my first thought was 'They've committed suicide.'

I immediately, instantly, went into action. Using money wherever possible, I dealt with the police, the media, and everyone else I had to, and was able to successfully ensure that the story was reduced to a brief news item about a straightforward accident.

Being that Maria was Catholic, I doubted that she could have initiated the suicide. It never was determined which one of them was behind the wheel at the time of the accident.

In my own mind, I mapped out a whole fantasy about how they had somehow doctored the accelerator and set the car in motion while they were in the back seat embracing and smiling lovingly at each other as the car careened into oblivion. This seemed like the best farewell gift that I could give them.

Appeasing Maria's family was no easy matter. I had to use all the influence I could muster to convince them to withdraw their allegation that K had killed their daughter. It required a huge sum of money. In business, image is everything. The situation gave me a deep appreciation for the old Japanese saying 'the life of an official is an unenviable one.' One has to put up with all sorts of humiliations when one is in the service of another."

This is the gist of the story that Mr. Tatsumi told me that day.

"Has Maria put a curse on my granddaughter because she still hates me so much for giving K the order to go home?"

I shook my head. "No," I said.

"That's not what's happening. I think Maria was reborn as a Japanese person because she wants so much to be together with Mr. K again. This one-pointed determination is the root cause of her reincarnating in Japan. She isn't here to cause Masami unhappiness or suffering. In fact, since Masami is a kind of 'duplicate' of herself, I imagine that she actually wants her to be happy.

"Unfortunately, though, the result of the situation is that Masami is miserable. This isn't about being cursed or not being cursed; it's about the fact that reincarnates always carry some amount of baggage with them from their previous lifetime that inevitably brings about this kind of situation.

"The main point here is that Maria's deep attachment needs to be extinguished. We can expiate the manifestation of Maria that is inside Masami by performing a *Gedatsu* (Liberation) service. If we then conduct a *Meitoku* service for Maria, who has now been brought into the spiritual dimension by *Gedatsu*, she might even become one of Maria's guardian angels who looks out for her happiness."

"I implore you to do whatever you can to make that happen."

At the present time, Masami is in the process of reverting back to her normal self. She is studying hard at school and diligently practicing her piano.

Maria was an up-and-coming pianist in Manila. I expect that Masami will come to exhibit the same degree of proficiency.

In the end, there is still one thing that I don't know. And that is, how does Mr. K figure in all this now? I imagine that he has been reborn somewhere as well. Is he in Japan? Is he in the Philippines? (He'll probably make his whereabouts known to me sooner or later.)

Formerly Caucasian

Over the years I have encountered many instances where a person reincarnates as a Japanese person from some other nationality.

But these reincarnations were rarely from Caucasian to Japanese. Most of the cases involved a person who had belonged to another Asian ethnic group in his or her former lifetime.

Recently, however, I've started to see examples that may represent the phenomenon of Caucasian to Japanese rebirth. Here is one of them.

Consultation Letter
Takako Miyagawa
S City
Age 34

My eldest son Shin'ichi (born July 13, 1987) began waking up in terror about two years ago. It happens an hour or two after he goes to sleep. Suddenly, he jumps up out of bed screaming and starts sleepwalking while he's crying.

It seems like he's having a nightmare, and he starts speaking words that we can't quite make out. Then, in the end, he yells clearly in Japanese, "Don't kill me! Don't kill me!" He looks absolutely terrified. I try to pick him up and hold him, but he twists and struggles and won't settle down.

This goes on for three or four nights a week. It takes 30 or 40 minutes before we can quiet him enough so that he goes back to sleep. Then the next day he's exhausted, and sleeps more than half the day.

We ask him about it, but he's only able to give us bits and pieces of information. What we've been able to gather is that it seems there is a group of men chasing after him trying to kill him. When we press him too hard it sends him into these fits again, so we don't want to ask him so much.

Right now his physical and intellectual development is normal, but we are afraid that if this behavior pattern continues it will do some kind of damage. Recently we have become more and more worried. He's had a slight tendency to stutter since he was little, but now it's becoming more pronounced. He's gotten very quiet and he isn't playful and childlike. We are starting to get concerned that these might be signs of autism.

We think his problems may be caused by spiritual interference of some kind. Please help save him. We beg you from the bottom of our hearts.

I haven't yet met the child in question. I did meet with his mother, and she repeated what is written here. There was one thing she said that really caught my attention. Apparently, he doesn't react negatively when he watches fight scenes in Japanese movies, even if many people are killed. He enjoys these kinds of movies just like other kids.

However, when he sees a murder scene in an American movie, especially a crime movie in which there are guns, he freaks out. He gets afraid and can't bear to watch. He goes into a panic and turns away, immediately changing the channel or running out of the room.

As I questioned her further she made the connection that the first time he had a fit, which had happened when he was very young, was after watching a violent American movie. The movie may have triggered his behavior. She said he was particularly sensitive to the sound of gunshots —they terrified him.

The stuttering is interesting. A slight stammer is something we often find in people who have reincarnated from another culture. Or we may find that they are especially taciturn. (Alternatively, they may show a special aptitude for their former language. Masami Fujio was very good at English.) This may have something to do with the brain's language center of the former incarnation. I came to the conclusion that Shin'ichi had either been an American or had American heritage. Or he may have been a Japanese person who emigrated to the West and then died an unnatural death there. One reason I think so is because the language that he spoke in his sleep, the one that the Miyagawas couldn't quite make out, was inflected in a way that sounded to them like English. And there's one more thing. What he liked to eat. He didn't want to eat rice; instead, he wanted things like bread and cheese. (And he was the only person in his family who exhibited these dietary preferences.) Now, there aren't any direct descendants of the Miyagawa line who ever emigrated to the West. Though there may have been some distant relative in generations past who did so.

I am still in the process of investigating this case clairvoyantly.

Past Life Memories

In my work, I do not conduct investigations into the past life memories of reincarnates the way that Dr. Stevenson does, like the ones he describes in his book *Children Who Remember Previous Lives*. My primary objective is always to figure out how to untie the destiny relationship between the former incarnation and the present one. Past life memories are just one of the keys that helps to unlock the mystery of what that relationship is in any given case. Though the past life memories that arise may be of interest to me, I don't pursue those memories in order to satisfy my curiosity. For me, these past life memories are nothing more than a supplemental tool to my clairvoyance.

It follows that the data I collect are not as startling and remarkable as those of Dr. Stevenson. Here is an example of his work from the aforementioned book:

> Sometimes the children act as if they have been snatched without warning from the body of an adult and thrust into that of a helpless child. When Celal Kapan, a subject in Turkey, began to speak, almost his first words were: "What am I

doing here? I was at the port." When he could say more, he described details in the life of a dockworker who had fallen asleep in the hold of a ship that was being loaded. Unfortunately, a crane operator who did not know he was there allowed a heavy oil drum to drop on him, killing him instantly. From the evidence of the case, one might say that this sleeping man regained consciousness in the body of a two-year-old child. These cases remind me of the case of a woman who had a stroke and became unconscious while playing bridge. When she regained consciousness several days later, her first words were: "What's trumps?"

...The children show differing expressions of emotion when they speak about the previous lives. Some speak of them with detachment, as if they are referring to far-off things, but the majority show a continuing strong involvement with the remembered people and events. Some weep as they talk about the previous life, others angrily denounce murderers who ended it. Teasing adults and siblings have brought some subjects to tears by falsely telling them that a spouse, other relative, or close friend of the previous personality was ill or had died.[iii]

My data doesn't include the accounts of reincarnates whose past life memories are as vivid as these are.

The fact that the objective of my investigations is not

---

iii. Ian Stevenson, *Children Who Remember Previous Lives*, p. 105

the past life memories themselves does not fully account for this difference. There is another reason as well.

And that is the fact that past life memories tend to be most vivid when one is young and to become more indistinct as one grows up.

Past life memories are probably most vivid right after one is born. As one matures, the mind must accommodate the immense amount of reality-based information that comes into it from the outside world. In other words, the mind becomes filled with a succession of new memories, and the old memories fade until they gradually disappear.

But the old memories are not extinguished completely. They go on to survive in the deeper layers of the mind, the subconscious and the unconscious. Over time, these are subsumed into the psychological trauma that impels our behavior.

The people whom I ordinarily would examine clairvoyantly are adults, or nearly so. Their past life memories have already faded. But given this, it is still true that in any number of cases, when I spend the time to question the person patiently and in detail, memories of their former lives are resuscitated. I'll give more examples of this later.

Chapter 2

On Being a Time Traveler in the Spiritual Dimensions

What I Found Out
by Using *Meitoku* Clairvoyance

I never would have imagined that there are as many people out there who are negatively driven reincarnates as there actually are.

I have been performing clairvoyant investigations for nearly 20 years. During that time, I've done an enormous number of them. Every once in a while I encounter a disembodied spirit so strange that I say to myself, "Now what in the world is this?" At first, I wasn't sure what it was about these spirits that made them so unusual. Later, I came to understand their strangeness was due to the fact that they themselves were negatively driven reincarnations of yet another individual.

I first came to this realization about three years ago while investigating the ancestral history of petitioners. In this work I use clairvoyance to identify the suffering spirits who are interfering in the lives of the people who come to me for help. I then help these disembodied beings to attain a state of liberation.

I use two different forms of clairvoyance.

The first I call *gedatsu* clairvoyance, or clairvoyance of liberation. This is the kind of clairvoyance I use to liberate any of the petitioner's immediate ancestors who may be causing problems in his or her life.

The second I call *meitoku* clairvoyance. This is a kind of clairvoyance that allows me to investigate more widely and deeply into a person's background. I use this kind of clairvoyance to identify any disembodied spirit who might be projecting interference into the petitioner's life.

I used *gedatsu* clairvoyance for the first 20 years that I performed these spiritual investigations. But *gedatsu* clairvoyance did not enable me to identify spirits as themselves negatively driven reincarnates. It was not until I began using *meitoku* clairvoyance that I was able to achieve that level of realization.

What is the difference?

In an investigation based on *gedatsu* clairvoyance I first ask the petitioner to provide me with a document which lists the immediate members of his or her family going back three generations. This is the sample I use to identify the ancestor who is creating the problem. I check out these beings clairvoyantly and almost always find the spirit who is causing trouble. I am able to do this whether or not the petitioner can give me a complete list, but it makes it easier to have one. Most people can trace their family back three generations with no problem.

I originally developed this method because I presumed that it would provide me with a wide enough net to catch the offending spirit. And, in most cases, the method was very successful.

But then one day I met up with such an unusual disembodied spirit that it changed everything...

"I Gave It All I Had"

Three years ago a middle-aged man named Mr. T came to me for a clairvoyant investigation.

T was the managing director of a second-rate company. He had graduated from the law department of a national university, and was the eldest son of a good family that had gone bankrupt three generations ago.

He was an affable, intellectually cultured gentleman, someone you might expect to be in a position of authority in a major firm. The truth is that he had started out working for a top-notch corporation. But then he had experienced a long string of bad luck.

It all started when his first manager, who doted on him, got sick and unexpectedly died.

The manager, Mr. S, had grown up in the same community as T, had gone to the same school, and had made him his protege. Mr. S was a real go-getter, and was very aggressive in whatever he did. Even though Mr. S had many rivals, he was clearly in the running to become president of the company some day. And the fact that this powerhouse had taken such a strong interest in T placed the younger man firmly on the road to success. In fact, T was the first of his age group to make it to chief clerk and his colleagues were already eyeing him enviously.

Then, soon after T had received this promotion, Mr. S died unexpectedly of a heart attack. Suddenly, everything that T tried to do seemed to go against him. His new manager, Mr. F, was a rival of Mr. S's, and began to treat

T coldly. Well, maybe he wasn't specifically singling him out, but he was naturally giving preferential treatment to his own favorites.

At one point, right after he had been promoted to section chief, Mr. T was assigned an important project. This was a real opportunity for him to get ahead. But then he was in a bad accident on the way home from work. The taxi he was riding in collided with another car and Mr. T suffered severe injuries that landed him in the hospital for three months. By the time he left the hospital, the project was already up and running, supervised by a rival of his who was executing the plan that T had devised. By the time he got back to work there was no place left for him in the operation and he never got any of the credit.

A number of years passed. T was given a temporary transfer to the office of a subsidiary that was in trouble. It was a managerial position and T's job was to restructure the business. Success in this venture would have improved his position in the company.

However, in a stroke of more bad luck, the company went into liquidation. The president of the company was not a team player, and he objected to everything that T tried to do to improve the situation of the business. The failure was entirely this other man's fault. But when things went bad, all the blame fell on T. He was seen as the commander of the losing army. Anything he might say sounded like an excuse or a recrimination.

T told me, "You know the expression 'pissing blood'. Well, I worked so hard that I actually did. I almost worked myself to death, but the employees ended up aligning themselves either with this guy or with me, and there was no way that I could unify the two sides. Anyway, in the end, I just didn't have what it takes. I gave it everything I had, but..." He dejectedly related his tale.

T was 52 years old. He lived with his wife, who was 48, and his only child, a daughter, 23. They had also had two sons, but both boys died in infancy.

His daughter was now of marriageable age. She had entertained a number of potential matches, but she was in ill health and nothing ever came of them.

There was a certain man she was fond of, and he wanted to marry her, but she didn't think she could make it because she just wasn't strong enough. Her menstrual cycle was very irregular and she was always coming down with something. There wasn't anything specifically wrong with her, but she always had one complaint or another— she had a cold, or a headache, or something. She had no stamina. She always felt exhausted and it was hard for her to get out of bed in the morning.

"I don't think there's any way that I could have a family. I don't know if I'll ever be able to get married," she would sometimes comment sadly. All the while she was forever taking Chinese herbal remedies and visiting one clinic or another, but nothing she did made her constitution stronger.

A person's destiny is determined by karma and by what we call in Japanese *innen*. *In* means cause and *nen* means condition. Thus, *innen* is the fundamental set of karmic causes and conditions that determines a person's fate. Many people use the term karma and *innen* interchangeably, but I believe this is a mistake. *Innen* are the conditions that determine a person's fate, whereas karma is the generative force that drives these conditions, or *innen*. Depending upon the strength of its manifestation, I characterize *innen* as being either minor or serious.

In trying to help a person resolve his or her life's difficulties, I will analyze the types of *innen* he or she has. Looking into the different kinds of *innen* that T had, I identified four main types:

1. The *innen of serious declining family fortune*
2. The *innen of inability to attain completion*
3. The *innen of conflict with family members*
4. The *innen of serious physical disability*, creating the possibility of an unnatural death

I can't imagine a worse line-up of *innen* than this.

First of all, T's overall family destiny is characterized by the *innen of serious declining family fortune*. With this kind of karmic conditioning, the fortunes of a family worsen from father to son, and so on from generation to generation. In the end, a family with this kind of *innen* is like grass without roots; the family eventually fades into extinction. Its members start to drift apart and disperse until the family structure itself finally dissolves.

The *innen of inability to attain completion* is a distinct outgrowth from the *innen of declining family fortune*. With this kind of karmic conditioning, it becomes impossible to finish things, no matter what one does and how hard one tries. One is never able to achieve success. This is also called 'the destiny of non-fruition' because it is like a blossom which appears but never bears fruit, or, should it bear fruit, is destined to be picked by someone else. Or to wither on the branch.

This is the karmic reason it had proven impossible for

Mr. T to achieve success, no matter how much talent he had and no matter how hard he had worked.

The *innen of conflict with family members* is an unhappy one that causes violent dissension among parents and their children, brothers and sisters, and all forms of family relations. It leads to senseless, hateful family confrontations. People get angry with each other and fight for the most trivial of reasons. Then when something major like the distribution of an inheritance is involved, the family situation can escalate into a deadly mess.

If T had been able to have more children, his relationship with them probably would have been marred by conflict. I suspect that there may have been some kind of family tragedy.

The fact that both of his male children died when they were little is a result of the combination of this specific *innen* with that of declining family fortune.

In similar fashion, his daughter's physical weakness and inability to marry come from the same sources. If she did marry, chances are she would end up getting divorced or she would be unable to bear children. In other words, the interaction of these different kinds of *innen* is acting in concert to bring about the possible extinction of the T family within this generation.

What about T's siblings? If we asked, I imagine we'd discover that they are all in comparable circumstances.

The fact that Mr. T was in a car accident and almost died as a result of his injuries is because he has the *innen of unnatural death*. It's a miracle that he survived. The next time something happens I doubt he'll be so lucky.

In order to find out where all these negative *innen*

came from, I entered into the deep state of meditative absorption from which I am able to clairvoyantly see into a person's background.

I soon encountered a disembodied spirit who was projecting negative energy onto T.

I questioned T about the being I had discovered.

"Do you know if there was someone in your family three generations ago who died an unnatural death?"

"Yes, I think I know who you mean. It was my great-grandfather. He was the person who squandered away all of our fortune."

When I tried to divine the karmic relationship between these two, I saw that T's karmic profile was almost identical to that of his great-grandfather. There was only one type of *innen* that T hadn't inherited from his ancestor, the *innen of marital discord*. The rest were all the same.

"Our family was among the most prominent landholders in all of G prefecture," T told me. "It's said that our estates were so large you could walk for seven and a half miles in any direction and never step onto another family's property. Then my great-grandfather was persuaded by some hangers-on to invest in the silkworm industry, and he ended up suffering huge losses. In order to get back what he lost, he kept trying his hand at one failed enterprise after another until he managed to lose practically everything. In the end, I heard he finally committed suicide by hanging himself."

So, as a result of receiving negative influence from the spirit of his great-grandfather, T was inheriting all of this bad karma. In Szondian terminology, he was experiencing 'the repetition' of his great-grandfather's 'fate'. In Kiriyama terminology, I would say he was experiencing 'the repetition of karma'.

I explained what I had seen to Mr. T.

"Pardon me?" He looked very concerned. "Does this mean I'm also going to hang myself?"

"No, that's not what it means at all. Now that we understand what is causing your problems we can fix them. So it's going to be all right. Here's what we have to do. I have to help your great-grandfather's spirit attain liberation and you have to do everything you can to cut off this inherited karma."

"Of course. Please help me in whatever way you can."

I nodded my assent.

I soon conferred a posthumous Buddhist name on his great-grandfather, and started to conduct the proper rituals to liberate his spirit.

But, wait a minute...

Something really strange was going on.

Disembodied spirits almost always attain a certain state of liberation the first time I conduct the proper rituals for them, no matter how strong their vengeful energy. In rare instances, a spirit's hostility is so strong that it takes a second ceremony to release them. But this doesn't happen often.

This time, however, even though I performed the ritual for the great-grandfather two times, something was still there. The vengeful energy hadn't disappeared.

"That's weird," I thought, puzzled.

This had never happened before. I re-entered the profound state of meditative absorption that affords me spiritual sight. I went into it very deeply.

A Strange Complex of Hostile Negativity

"My goodness," I thought as I realized that there was something else hidden behind the vengeful spirit of the great-grandfather. It was another configuration of negative energy. And this vengefulness was even stronger than his was. Together they formed a strange complex of hostile negativity.

"So that's it!" I exclaimed to myself. "The great-grandfather himself was a negatively driven reincarnation!"

I went after the negative energy of the disincarnate entities with all of my power.

This led to the discovery of some surprising information.

The great-grandfather was the reincarnation of a man who had lived and killed himself two generations before the great-grandfather was born. However, the first man was not an immediate relative of the T family. In fact, he had not been related to them at all. Instead, he was just someone who developed a serious grudge against them. He hated them so much that he had hung himself over it. He was born into the T family after he killed himself.

I called T to my side and asked him the following question.

"Did you ever hear about someone who bore your family such an enormous grudge that he killed himself over it? He would have been alive two or three generations before your great-grandfather."

T thought about this for a little while before he

answered.

"You know, I did hear about something that happened a very long time ago. I'm not sure of all the facts, but I heard something about a man who had borrowed money from my family and wasn't able to pay it back. As a result, he lost his farm. He blamed my family, and squirreled himself away in our barn where he ended up hanging himself. He wrote 'I curse this family for seven generations' on a piece of paper and pasted it to the wall of the barn. The family razed the building to the ground soon after he killed himself."

So what happened is that this man reincarnated into the T family (as T's great-grandfather) for the specific purpose of destroying them by squandering away all their money.

If this poor spirit was not helped to attain a state of liberation, the great-grandfather would never be completely free, and, consequently, T would continue to suffer from his negative spiritual interference and be unable to cut through his own karma.

"So this is how this came about!" I realized, and took a deep breath.

This was an extraordinarily valuable experience.

It was the experience that resulted in my beginning to practice *meitoku* clairvoyance.

Up until that point, I had been using *gedatsu* clairvoyance to spiritually investigate the members of the petitioner's family within the three-generation framework of the lineage document. In *meitoku* clairvoyance, I move outside that framework and go back as many generations as I need to clear the interference. In terms of time frame, this kind of investigation can span one hundred or more years. In terms of space, it can include hundreds of spirits. It is a job that requires a very systematic approach.

This is why I say I am a kind of time traveler. I am a time traveler in the spiritual dimension.

Last year, right before reaching retirement age, T secured an executive position within the company. Around the same time, his daughter regained her health and got married. She is now expecting a baby. Some late-blooming buds are finally about to flower for this family!

Vertical and Horizontal Karma vs. Diagonal Karma

Up until that time I subscribed to the theory that there was what I called vertical karma and horizontal karma, and that human destiny consists of these two elements.

This is illustrated on the following page.

The locus of the 'self' lies at the point where the two modalities of vertical and horizontal karma intersect.

Vertical karma is that which is inherited from one's ancestors.

Horizontal karma is that which is carried over from former lifetimes.

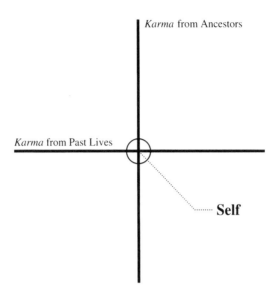

It isn't necessary to go into a detailed explanation of vertical karma. These are the karmic causes and conditions that everyone receives from their ancestors through their parents. It's obvious that we inherit characteristics like physical appearance, constitution, mental aptitude, and psychological tendencies from our parents. I don't expect anyone to dispute this.

But what about horizontal karma?

This is where it gets difficult. There may be some people who want to dispute the existence of this kind of karmic inheritance. These are the same people who don't believe in past lives and the like. So let us address this issue.

When we talk about inheriting causes and conditions from our ancestors, how do we determine which of these came from which of our ancestors? So many people have come before us. Merely in terms of direct descendants, the previous three generations provide us with 14 ancestors and the past five generations include 60.

Masahiro Yasuoka, an eminent scholar of Chinese thought, has noted that if we go back 20 generations we find over a million ancestors and if we go back 30 generations we have over a billion. Furthermore, the science of genetics tells us that a given characteristic of a mouse that lived 5,000 generations ago may be manifest in the animal's present-day descendant. Five thousand mouse generations are roughly equivalent to 10 human generations. This means that specific characteristics (karma) of a person who lived 10 generations ago can re-emerge in his or her contemporary descendant.

But which one of our ancestors did we get any given karma from? What particular kind of karma did we get from which specific person? These are the questions we are faced with. We each have thousands of ancestors who lived 10 generations ago. How do we know where our own individual karma came from?

Now, if we could survey the personalities of all these ancestors we would find that some of them were outstandingly virtuous people and that some of them were horrible human beings, maybe even murderers. Some were bums and some were millionaires. So whose karma did we inherit?

Think about the different children in the same family. They all have the same parents and ancestors but they don't get the same karma; everyone has their own individual set of karmic causes and conditions. How is such karmic differentiation produced?

By way of explanation, let us imagine a scenario of five siblings.

Eldest Son, A

He starts out in this poor family but industriously manages to build a huge fortune within his lifetime. He is active in public affairs and well respected in the community. He lives a long life.

Second Son, B

He is an ordinary sort of fellow, not particularly good or bad one way or the other. In the end, he dies of cancer.

Eldest Daughter, C

She has bad luck with her marriages. Due to the strong presence of the *innen of serious marital discord*, her first marriage ends in divorce and her second one is unhappy. She is unable to bear children.

Third Son, D

He has the *innen of unnatural death* and, while still young, gets in a fight and is murdered.

Second Daughter, E

She is blessed with the karma of a good marriage and decent children. She leads a happy life then dies of a stroke.

Imagine that this group of siblings exists. (Actually, it does.)

The third son, D, is probably bemoaning his fate, thinking, "Why am I the only one who had to die an unnatural death."

And the eldest daughter, C, is probably off pouting

somewhere, grumbling about ending up with such lousy marriage karma.

These brothers and sisters were born from the same parents and they all have the same ancestors, so why are they all so different? The key to understanding this is horizontal karma.

Let us say for argument's sake that the eldest son led a virtuous and happy life the previous time around. He was generous with his possessions and well respected by his community. His good deeds create a karmic bond between him and a similarly virtuous ancestor who lived a number of generations before him.

Similarly, let us assume that the third son, D, in his last lifetime, was a wild, violent man. He performed many negative deeds that hurt other people, including murder. This causes him to connect to an ancestor who had the same kind of karma and lived a number of generations before him, one who had the karma to commit murder, and to be executed, the *innen of unnatural death*.

The second son, the eldest daughter, in fact all of them, follow the same pattern: they live a life similar to the one they did before and this connects them to an ancestor who had types of *innen* similar to theirs.

So even though these brothers and sisters may come from the same set of parents, they have each lived individually diverse lives in the past. Consequently, they have correspondingly different karmic make-ups in this lifetime. This follows the theory of vertical and horizontal karma.

But then again...

What I learned from utilizing *meitoku* clairvoyance is that sometimes another line of karma, a diagonal line, can suddenly come arcing into that of vertical karma. This line can appear abruptly, from an unexpected direction. Therefore, I also refer to this kind of karma as 'shooting-star' karma.

In diagonal karma a reincarnate enters your vertical karma stream who is not related to you by birth, a person who is a total stranger. Just like a shooting star. Furthermore, this shooting star may in fact be no other than you yourself.

Realizing this was a profound shock to me.

Diagonal Karma — T Family

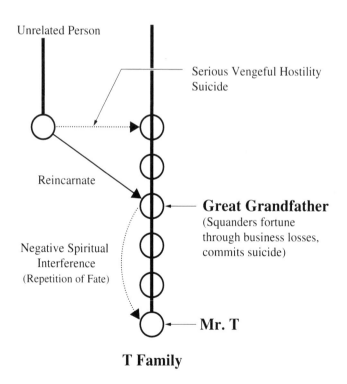

Unrelated Person

Serious Vengeful Hostility
Suicide

Reincarnate

Great Grandfather
(Squanders fortune
through business losses,
commits suicide)

Negative Spiritual
Interference
(Repetition of Fate)

Mr. T

T Family

I now understand upon reflection that grasping this information was the vital link that enabled me to complete Agon-shu's method of liberation from negative karma.

As noted, a person's rebirth, or reincarnation, exerts an enormous influence on his or her karmic make-up. Actually, reincarnation is more than a big influence. It's not an exaggeration to say that reincarnation is the fundamental condition of a person's karmic constitution. It is impossible to achieve liberation from negative karma without recognizing this fact.

The reason I myself started Buddhist practice was because I was searching for a way to attain liberation from karma. I pursued this goal assiduously for more than 50 years. And here, at last, was a complete system.

The Agamas contain a number of sutras in which Shakyamuni Buddha addresses the matter of reincarnation. Looking back on it today, I must have read those passages hundreds of times and I know I lectured about them repeatedly to other people. And yet, I hadn't realized their true meaning.

The Buddha's teachings were not merely expositions of the fact that reincarnation exists. Shakyamuni also expounded on the deep relationship between reincarnation, on the one hand, and the liberation from karma and attaining Buddhahood, on the other. This information enabled me to realize the true meaning of these teachings.

The Role of Reincarnation in Extreme Misfortune

Destroying One's Own Chances at Marriage

Takako Hayashi
Age 28

I've been involved in a series of matchmaking interviews [in the custom of arranged marriage]. In my own mind, I definitely want to get married, but before any successful conclusion to the process I always say or do something to mess it up.

The more enthusiastic the other party gets, the more averse I become. Once I really liked a guy and started to feel like I wanted to get serious with him. We were almost ready to get married, and then all I could see were his faults and in the end I couldn't stand him.

I myself have a lot of shortcomings, and I'm definitely not someone who should be criticizing anybody else, but I always do, and I always wreck my relationships. I keep repeating this same thing over and over again.

I get very sad when I think that, if this continues, I may never get married. Please help me.

Takako Hayashi works as a pre-school teacher. There's something sort of dark about her, but she's smart and above average in appearance, even rather beautiful.

The troubles that she wrote me about in this letter had been going on for quite a few years. She did meet men she was attracted to, but as soon as she got to know them better she began to feel a growing sense of anxiety and distaste, and eventually did something to undermine the progression of their relationship. Sometimes she'd say or do something completely unconscious that would turn the guy off.

If her prospective partner went to hold her hand or touch her in any way, she'd feel totally revolted. But even though she didn't want men to touch her, she definitely wasn't a homosexual. She sincerely wanted to get married.

It's been over three years since Ms. Hayashi first sent me a consultation letter. During this period there have been two or three times where I have counseled her to accept a certain proposal of marriage. But she spoiled every one of these chances through her indecisiveness. After each of these episodes she has come to me to apologize.

In the course of working with her, I discovered that disembodied spirits was negatively affecting Ms. Hayashi, and I did about ten spiritual liberation ceremonies to help her. But, even with that, she still couldn't quite manage to complete the marriage process. She'd get close, but then she'd become anxious and repulsed and, in the end, screw up whatever marriage negotiations were going on.

Last year, I realized that Ms. Hayashi was a negatively driven reincarnation whose situation was similar to Mr. T's. I discovered that there was a female spirit lurking behind one of the disembodied spirits who was, in turn, affecting her.

It turns out that the lurking spirit was that of a woman who was a previous incarnation of Ms. Hayashi herself. This woman came to an unhappy end after she married a man who betrayed her terribly. She was an only child and her husband was adopted into her family to carry on the family name. He was only after her money, and as soon as her parents died he began to show his true colors. He took control of all the family property, and moved another woman into the house and carried on with her right out in the open like he was purposefully trying to hurt his wife. In the end the betrayed woman killed herself. She lived three generations ago, and was a member of the main branch of Ms. Hayashi's family.

I was able to help the spirit of the dead woman achieve liberation through a *meitoku* service.

In September of last year, Ms. Hayashi successfully completed a marriage agreement and happily went to the altar. "This time I was able to openly trust the other person," she confided in the thank-you letter she sent to me.

If we hadn't been able to liberate the spirit of the troubled spirit Ms. Hayashi probably would not have been able to get married in this lifetime. And even if she had endured her misgivings and tied the knot with someone, she probably would have been as miserable as she was the last time around. (Even if she didn't commit suicide.)

Incidentally, Ms. Hayashi was also an only child.

Misunderstood and Alone

Tetsuo Okuda
Age 27

I graduated from college three years ago, and began a career as a businessman.

It has always been difficult for me to make conversation, and I have trouble interacting comfortably with other people. That's one reason I opted to study technology in school and to work in a technology-related field. But my relationship with the other people at work isn't good.

Everyone always seems to misinterpret what I'm trying to say. I can't seem to get people to understand what I mean.

I always find myself sitting alone at lunch, and no one ever asks me out for a drink after work.

I'm working as hard as everybody else, but I have trouble concentrating on what I'm doing because I'm always thinking about why I can't get along with my co-workers.

All the women at work are friendly to the other guys but they avoid me like the plague.

Is there something about me that is really so offensive to other people?

I hate going to work so much that I just can't stand it. What in the world should I do?

I receive numerous letters chronicling similar complaints. Many of them come from people like working women and students. Needless to say, not all of these people are the victims of spiritual interference nor are they all negatively driven reincarnations.

But when the problems are the result of reincarnation, they are serious and difficult to resolve.

Here is a list of typical characteristics that may signal someone is a negatively driven reincarnation.

One exhibits:

1. Strong feelings of suspicion and wariness.

2. Strong feelings that one is being treated unjustly, is being persecuted. Believing that someone is always out to get one.

   Feeling like one is under attack.

3. Obsessions; obstinately holding on to one certain thing.

4. Strong feelings of frustration. The belief, from the start, that things aren't going to work out. Then when things do become problematic, over-reacting with something like impulsive thoughts of suicide.

5. Strong feelings of isolation. Deep fear of strangers, coupled with a great selectivity towards other people.

6. A schizophrenic-type personality.

These are the main characteristics.

For example, in the case of Tetsuo Okuda, the truth is that his colleagues are not particularly against him. Much of what he is experiencing is the result of his own projection, and this is resulting in his increasing isolation. His co-workers are merely reacting to his odd guardedness and suspicious manner, his paranoia. It is only natural for them to gradually draw away from him and to exclude him from their friendly banter.

It's not surprising that over time he would straggle behind his peer group. And it is hard to imagine him achieving much happiness. Rather, it's more likely that he will sink further and further into unhappiness.

Psychologically speaking, Tetsuo Okuda is suffering from a typical kind of predestined neurosis. Sigmund Freud defines neurosis as an irresistible force in the unconscious that causes a person to act in a certain way. In this case, the neurosis causes the person to become frustrated and fail whenever he or she is trying to accomplish something.

Freud called this force that lurks in the unconscious 'repetition compulsion'. When he investigated the childhood of people who had it, Freud discovered a consistent pattern. He found that the subject was always defeated by having things spoiled right before he attained his objective.

For example, the subject might be strong academically and doing well in school. But then, when he had to take an important exam, something would happen to make him fail; he'd get sick or forget an answer that he really knew. Or maybe he was chosen to compete in a big sports event, but would sprain his ankle right before the start of the game and be unable to play. Or maybe there was something a child had wanted for a really long time and right before her father was going to get it for her, she acted up and made him so angry he changed his mind. In other words, something defeating always happens to insure that he or she will not be successful in achieving his or her desire.

In some cases the person appears to create the situation and in some it seems to spring from some external, fated, irresistible force. But, in either event, the result is failure.

On the surface, it may seem like a 'fated, irresistible force'. But, as Freud posits, somewhere in the back of the person's mind, in the depths of their unconscious, there is a self-destructive mechanism in place that is forcing them to move in the direction of failure.

Freud is not alone in his opinion; other psychologists agree with him. For example, Menninger also posits that certain people have the syndrome of self-destruction.

Let us paraphrase some of Freud's comments on this matter:

> There reaches a point in the psychoanalytic process where this type of patient starts to complain that the therapy is only making them worse or that it is completely ineffective. Contrary to their complaints, this is often evidence that the therapy is gradually starting to have a beneficial effect and we must persuade the patient to continue treatment.
>
> Then, just when we are both certain that the patient has reached the brink of attaining a measure of happiness and relief from what may have been years of suffering, the patient starts to encounter real difficulties. As the patient starts to feel a sense of ease, unexpected things suddenly begin to occur. For example, he has a fight with his superiors at work and gets fired, or he argues with his spouse and talks about divorce. He gets injured in a car accident. Or a promising business deal goes sour. These events, which may at first

appear to be mere coincidence but are in fact self-generated, will throw the patient back into a state of misery. The effects of the treatment and the imminent attainment of happiness evaporate. The patient comes to the conclusion that, just has he predicted, the therapy is a failure.

When we investigate this kind of patient's childhood, we soon discover a pattern of failure that has been in place as long as he can remember. All experiences of intimacy have been undermined; as soon as he approaches a state of closeness with another person, conflicts arise that end the relationship. The patient ends up enfolded in loneliness. He may find a suitable marriage partner but at some point before the wedding there will be some sort of anxiety-produced crisis that will break them apart. Or the patient will not be able to hold down a job because he always creates divisiveness among co-workers and superiors wherever he works. And so on and so on.

It is as though the patient's conscious mind is being controlled by some strange power. The patient may be dimly aware that he is carrying the conviction that he is incapable of attaining complete fulfillment and happiness in this lifetime.

When we mine down into the patient's unconscious we discover that, in fact, he is holding onto a strong internal belief, of which he is not fully conscious, that he is being controlled by a destiny that predetermines his unhappiness and that he has no control over this power. Furthermore, he reacts

to the proximity of happiness with great anxiety—
it makes him feel that he is no longer himself.
And, as a result, he acts out his fear in unconsciously self-destructive behavior.

Freud claims that this kind of person has a 'repetition
compulsion'. But, in my humble opinion, this theory does
nothing more than simply identify and name the symptoms
of the real problem.

The important question here is where this 'repetition
compulsion' comes from, and Freud's theory does nothing
to elucidate the answer.

I have no doubt that this force is a distinctive characteristic of negatively driven reincarnates, of people who
have been reborn with seriously unresolved issues from
their pasts.

I believe this kind of person's self-destructive behavior
is attributable to the fact he is "carrying the conviction that
he is incapable of attaining complete fulfillment and
happiness in this lifetime."

And that this conviction comes from memories of the
scathing frustration and failure that he experienced in his
past life.

"When we mine down into the patient's unconscious
we discover that, in fact, he is holding onto a strong
internal belief, of which he is not fully conscious, that he
is being controlled by a destiny that predetermines his
unhappiness and that he has no control over this power."
I believe that one reason this conviction arises is because a
negatively driven reincarnate has often suffered an unnatural death in his former incarnation. Or that he ended his

former days in a state of extreme misery. The bitter resentment he experienced in the past is the generative factor for his rebirth into this world. It is not surprising that his unconscious harbors expectations of bad luck and unhappiness.

Even if the person doesn't recall past life memories of specific events he won't be able to erase the overall impression of having been an unhappy person, an impression that stays with him into the present. This basic fact underlies the various characteristics of the reincarnate listed above.

And here are the two reasons why I used the heading "The Role of Reincarnation in Extreme Misfortune" at the head of this section.

1. Because I have found that, externally, extremely unfortunate people 'repeat the fate' of the extremely unfortunate person they were in their last lifetime, and

2. Because I have found that, internally, extremely unfortunate people possess a psychological tendency towards self-destruction that they carry with them from before.

The combination of these two principles causes the person who has them to experience great suffering.

If you have god-given talents but seem to experience a lot of bad luck even when you really apply yourself (or if you have the desire to work hard but can't seem to get it together), then I'd like you to consider the possibility that you yourself might be a negatively driven reincarnate.

Why Do People Reincarnate?

What is the reason that people reincarnate?

Beginning with Edgar Cayce, many Western psychics seem to believe that human beings continue to be born and die in a process of gradual ascent (perfection) that leads them to God.

I'm afraid that I'm unable to agree with this assertion. In fact, I'm afraid that the opposite may be closer to the truth.

Dr. Ian Stevenson, in his book *Children Who Remember Previous Lives*, notes that "it seems that many reincarnates died untimely deaths."

This is similar to the conclusion that I have drawn from my own clairvoyant investigations. I find that most negatively driven incarnates seem to have ended their last lives in a state of bitter negativity and resentment.

So which of the above conclusions is correct?

Shakyamuni Buddha offers an explicit answer to this question. Let us look at one of the sutras in which he addresses the issue of human rebirth. This is an excerpt from the *Seniya Sutra* of the *Samyukta Agama*.

The Buddha's Answer: "The Continuation of Other Skandhas"

Thus have I heard. One time the Exalted One was dwelling in Rajagaha* in the Bamboo Grove at the Squirrels' Sanctuary*. The Wanderer* Seniya went to visit the Exalted One, and on coming to him saluted him courteously, and after the exchange of courtesies sat down at one side. So seated he said to the Exalted One:—

'Master Gotama, some time ago, on some former occasions, a number of sectarians of different views—shramanas*, brahmins*, charakas*, and monks, who were wanderers, had met together and were sitting in the Debating Hall, when this topic of talk arose':

'Purana Kassapa*, who has 500 followers, who is teacher of a crowd, a well-known and famous founder of theories, one in high repute among the manyfolk. Among his disciples are some wise ones and some ignorant ones. When speaking of a disciple who has passed away, who has made an end, he does not describe him in terms of rebirth saying: "So and so is reborn thus and thus." Makkhali of the Cowpen was there, who has 500 followers, who is teacher of a crowd, a well-known and famous founder of theories, one in high repute among the manyfolk. Among his disciples are some wise ones and some ignorant ones. When speaking of a disciple who has passed away, who has made an end, he does not describe him in terms of rebirth saying: "So and so is reborn thus and thus." Nata's Son the Unclothed was there, who has 500 followers, who is teacher of a crowd, a well-known and famous founder of theories, one in high repute among the manyfolk. Among his disciples are some wise ones and some ignorant ones. When speaking of a disciple who has passed away, who has made an end, he does not describe him in terms of rebirth saying: "So and so is reborn thus and thus." Sanjaya, Belatthi's Son was there, who has 500 followers, who is teacher of a crowd, a well-known and famous founder of theories, one in high repute among the manyfolk. Among his disciples are some wise ones and some ignorant ones. When speaking of a disciple who has passed away, who has made an end, he does not describe him in terms of rebirth saying: "So and so is reborn thus and thus." Kaccayana of the Pakuddhas was there, who has 500 followers, who is teacher of a crowd, a well-known and famous founder of theories, one in high repute among the manyfolk. Among his disciples are some wise ones and some ignorant ones. When speaking of a disciple who has passed away, who has made an end, he does not describe him in terms of rebirth saying: "So and so is reborn thus and thus." Ajita of the Haircloth was there, who has 500 followers, who is teacher of a crowd, a well-known and famous founder of theories, one in high repute among the manyfolk. Among his disciples are some wise ones and some ignorant ones. When speaking of a disciple who has passed away, who has made an end, he does not describe him in terms of rebirth saying: "So and so is reborn thus and thus."

'Now here is Gotama the Monk, who has a crowd of followers, who is teacher of a crowd, a well-known and famous founder of theories, one in high repute among the manyfolk. Among his disciples are some wise ones and some ignorant ones. When speaking of a disciple who has passed away, who has made an end, he describes his rebirth saying: "So and so is reborn thus and thus."

'Of this matter, master Gotama, I had doubt and wavering, and I thought: How is the teaching of Gotama the recluse to be understood in this matter?'

The Exalted One said to Seniya:

'It is enough to cause you bewilderment, Seniya, enough to cause you confusion. Seniya, you should know this. There are three different kinds of views.

'The first view teaches that the Self (Atman) exists only for this present lifetime. It does not declare what happens to the self after death.

'The second view teaches that the Self exists in this lifetime and continues after death.

'And then, Seniya, there is another view.

'The third view teaches that the Self neither

exists in this lifetime nor continues after death.

'The first view is known as the theory of Annihilation*. This is how it is known.

'The second view is known as the theory of Eternalism*. This is how it is known.

'The third view is known as the theory of the Norm (of the middle way). This is how it is known. It is the Right View of the Tathagata. It teaches how to cut craving, how to separate from desire and extinguish it in this very lifetime and thus attain Nirvana*.'

The Wanderer Seniya then solemnly said to the Exalted One:

'After listening to your replies, Exalted One, my bewilderment and confusion have increased.'

The Exalted One said to Seniya:

'It is enough to cause you more bewilderment, Seniya, enough to cause you more confusion. It is difficult for an untaught ordinary person to understand this. For this Dhamma, Seniya, is profound, hard to see and hard to understand, peaceful and sublime, unattainable by mere reasoning, subtle, to be experienced by the wise. It is hard for a sentient people to understand it when they hold another view, accept another teaching, approve of another teaching, pursue a different training, and follow a different teacher.'

And then Seniya spoke to Master Gotama again:

'Exalted One. At your side I have attained a mind of pure faith. I wish only to sit at your side and hear you teach the Dhamma so that my eyes may be purified by its wisdom.'

The Exalted One said to Seniya:

'So I shall question you about this in return, Seniya. Answer as you choose. What do you think, Seniya? Is the body permanent or impermanent?'

'Impermanent, master Gotama.'

'What do you think, Seniya? Is what is impermanent characterized by suffering or not?'

'It is characterized by suffering, master Gotama.'

'Now what is impermanent, what is suffering, what is of a nature to change*, is it proper to regard that thus: "This is mine. This am I. This is my self."'

'Surely not, master Gotama.'

'So seeing, Seniya, the well taught noble disciple holds the view that "This (body) is not mine. This am not I. This is not my self."

'Likewise, Seniya, what do you think? Are the feelings permanent or impermanent?...

'Are perceptions permanent or impermanent?...

'Are the mental formations permanent or impermanent?...

'Is consciousness permanent or impermanent?...'

'They are not, master Gotama.'

'So seeing, Seniya, the well taught noble disciple holds the view that "This is not mine. This am not I. This is not my self."

'Now, what do you think, Seniya? Does the Tathagata* regard the body as the self or not?'

'Surely not, master Gotama.'

'Does the Tathagata regard the self as having body or not?'

'Surely not, master Gotama.'

'Does the Tathagata regard the body as being in the self or not?'

'Surely not, master Gotama.'

'Does the Tathagata regard the self as being in the body or not?'

'Surely not, master Gotama.'

'Likewise, Seniya, does the Tathagata regard feeling ... perception ... mental formation ... consciousness...?'

'Surely not, master Gotama.'

'Now, Seniya, some of my disciples who hear these teachings are not able to understand them. They have not extinguished obscurations and realized infinite wisdom* and so do not attain Nirvana. Because they have not attained Nirvana they have not extinguished obscurations. Because they have not extinguished obscurations, when they die and leave behind the five aggregates (skandhas)* of this world, other skandhas continue to exist. This, Seniya, is why when speaking of a disciple who has passed away, who has made an end, I am able to describe his rebirth: "So and so is reborn thus and thus." It is because he has not extinguished obscurations that aggregates continue to exist.

'Now, Seniya, my disciples who do understand these teachings are able to extinguish obscurations and so do attain Nirvana. They have attained Nirvana because they have extinguished obscurations. Because they have extinguished craving, when they die and leave behind the five aggregates (*skandhas*) of this world, other skandhas do not continue to exist. This, Seniya, is why when speaking of a disciple who has passed away, who has made an end, I do not describe his rebirth: "So and so is reborn thus and thus." It is because he has extinguished his karma so aggregates do not continue to exist. This is how I respond when I am asked about such a disciple. He has extinguished all craving and has separated himself from clinging for a long period of time. He has attained right intention and liberation. He has reached to a state that is very difficult to attain.

'Seniya, this is what I have been teaching for a long time, about the excess of obscurations, the aggregation of obscurations, the arising of obscurations, and the root of obscurations. When one acquires infinite wisdom about obscurations, one attains Nirvana and suffering no longer arises.'

At that time the Wanderer Seniya's Dhamma Eye was opened. The Wanderer Seniya saw the Dhamma, attained the Dhamma, understood the Dhamma, fathomed the Dhamma; he crossed beyond doubt, did away with perplexity, gained intrepidity, and became independent of others in the Teacher's Dispensation.

Then he said to the Exalted One: 'I go to the Blessed One for refuge and to the Dhamma and to the Sangha of bhikkhus. I would receive the going forth under the Blessed One, I would receive the full admission.'

Then Seniya received the going forth under the Blessed One, and he received the full admission. And not long after his ordination the venerable Seniya, remaining alone and separate, earnest, ardent and strenuous, attained ere long to that supreme goal of the divine life for the sake of which clansmen rightly go forth from the home life into homelessness. He directly knew: Birth is destroyed, the holy life has been lived, what had to be done has been done, there is not more coming to any state of being. And the venerable Seniya became one of the arahants.

(That is what the Blessed One said. Seniya was satisfied and delighted in the Blessed One's words.)

Notes

* Rajagaha
  The capital of the kingdom of Magadha, present-day Rajgir.
* Bamboo Grove at the Squirrels' Sanctuary
  (*Venuvana-kalandaka-nivasa*)
  Seniya Bimbisara, the king of Magadha, donated the Bamboo Grove at the Squirrels' Sanctuary to Shakyamuni Buddha's religious order. Also known as the Bamboo Grove Monastery.
* The Wanderers

The members of the non-Buddhist religious sects which existed in India at the time of Shakyamuni. Also their followers. Alternatively referred to as the Sects of the Six Teachers, the Ninety-Six Schools, and the Six Schools of Philosophy.

* Shramana

A wanderer, ascetic, spiritual striver.

* Brahmin

The highest of the four castes in Indian society. The priests of Hinduism.

* Charaka

One of the non-Buddhist sects. There isn't much known about them.

* Purana Kassapa

The leader of one of the non-Buddhist sects, as are the other five teachers mentioned in this passage.

* The Doctrine of Annihilation

A doctrine that is the opposite of eternalism, one in which the world and the self are seen to be subject to extinction. In non-recognition of the law of cause and effect, the mistaken belief that death marks the final end of the individual. The belief that the self exists only for one lifetime, and that there are no consequences to either good or evil actions.

* The Doctrine of Eternalism

The doctrine that the world is eternal and changeless, not subject to extinction, and that the conditioned elements are eternal. This doctrine is based on the theory that the self (Atman), which is falsely perceived as eternal, continues after death.

* Nirvana

The Sanskrit form of the vernacular word *nibban*. Not easily explained, Nirvana is the particular realm of existence in which, having cut one's karma, one is liberated from cause and conditions. Synonymous with

'Attaining Buddhahood'. The attainment of Nirvana extinguishes future existence (future lifetimes, life after death); it severs the process of reincarnation. To the extent that one has not achieved Nirvana, one repeats human existence which is characterized by ignorance and suffering. When Shakyamuni attained Nirvana he became the Buddha. It is the ultimate goal of Buddhism.

* Principle of Change (Dependent Origination)
  The truth that nothing in this world is eternal. The principle of change arises from 'conditions'. Also known as the principle of causation.

* Tathagata
  This word can mean either Buddha or ideal sentient beings. In this sutra, both meanings are used.

* Infinite Wisdom
  Supreme wisdom; the wisdom which procures Nirvana (liberation).

* Skandha
  Aggregate. Bundle.
  The five skandhas are form (general materiality, or the physical body), perception, feeling, mental constituents, and consciousness (these last four are mental functions). These are the five psychophysical elements that comprise the human being.

Commentary

This Sutra contains teachings given to Seniya about existence after death.

One day Seniya, who was a seeker in one of the non-Buddhist sects, came to visit the Buddha.

Seniya told the Buddha that he had recently attended a gathering of monks and brahmins that was held at the debating hall. The assembled were discussing the fact that

Purana Kassapa and five other masters of the non-Buddhist sects would not explain what happens to their disciples after they die. Only the Buddha explains what happens to his disciples after they die.

Seniya wanted to know on what basis the Buddha explains what happens after a person dies, which is something that no human being can know.

In response, Shakyamuni Buddha brings up three doctrines that were in vogue at the time. The first two doctrines he mentions are that of Annihilation and that of Eternalism, both of which he says are wrong. Next he cites the doctrine of Immutable Karma, which he also says is not the truth. He goes on to say that the true doctrine is that of Dependent Origination.

The Buddha says that because existence arises from causes and conditions the cycle of birth and death continues as long as causes and conditions exist. Existence (the self) cannot exist outside of causes and conditions, so cannot exist forever (as eternalism would have it). Unless causes and conditions are extinguished, death does not bring the cessation of existence (as the annihilationists claim). The Buddha says it is also untrue that karma can be determined without causes and conditions (as per the theory of immutable karma). Existence (the self) arises because of causes and conditions. It can only be extinguished through the extinction of causes and conditions.

Thus, being (the self) continues as long as it possesses causes and conditions. If one performs spiritual practice based on the principle of dependent origination one will extinguish one's causes and conditions and stop the cycle of life and death and enter the state of Nirvana. The

Buddha taught that this is the right view of the Tathagata.

However, the Buddha went on to say that only a few of his disciples had fully realized this truth because most of them continued to be deluded by attachment to the idea of the self. This karma causes them to be born into another body of five skandhas (as they continue into their next dimension of existence), even after they had lain aside the body of five skandhas they had while here on earth. Their karma prevents them from escaping reincarnation. The intense craving (*tanha*) of self-attachment causes them to reincarnate.

There is much variation in the degree of self-attachment among individuals. Examining these variations gives a clear indication of what kind of existence the individual is headed towards and where he or she will be reborn. The Buddha says that he can see that this disciple is going to be reborn over here, and that that disciple is going to be reborn over there. He can tell which disciple is going to be born when and where and in what kind of circumstance after he or she dies according to the kind of self-attachment he or she has exhibited while here on earth.

But in cases where the practitioner is successful in extinguishing the attachment to self and therefore no longer has the causes and conditions to transmigrate, the Buddha does not explain what is going to happen to such a sage after death.

Receiving these teachings purified Seniya's Dharma Eye and he took refuge with the Buddha. In the end he attained the enlightenment of an Arahant.

The above summarizes the content of the sutra, but the

Agon Shu's Sohonzan Sohonden Shakazan Daibodai-ji, the main temple of Agon Buddhism in Kyoto, Japan.

most essential statement is "Because they have not extinguished self-attachment, another body of skandhas arises and continues after they leave behind their physical body." This is the main point of the teaching.

Another sutra offers an explanation about this other body that may be easier to understand. The following passage is paraphrased from *Sayings about the Unrevealed*, sutra 44 of the *Samyutta Nikaya*.

The Fire Continues to Burn Even after the Fuel Is Gone

This sutra is an account of the time that Vacchagotta the Wanderer came to visit the Buddha and questioned him about what happens after death.

One day the Wanderer Vacchagotta came to see Shakyamuni Buddha who was staying at the Bamboo Grove Monastery. He requested teachings on the matter of what happens after one dies.

"How then, master Gotama? Is the self the same as the body?"

"It is not revealed, Vaccha, that the self is the same as the body"

"How then, master Gotama? Is the self one thing and the body another?"

"It is not revealed, Vaccha, that the self is one thing and the body another."

"Now the Exalted One says it is not revealed whether the self and the body are the same thing or another. But I have heard that the Exalted One teaches the disciples where one or another of them will be reborn and so on. On what basis do you give such a teaching? When a person dies their body becomes smoke, so there must be something to form the person's fixed reappearance in the next existence. That something must be the spirit, and so it follows that there must be a spirit as distinct from the physical body."

"No, Vacchagotta, that is not for certain. I teach that if the self is a conditioned one, then it will reappear in one of the five realms of existence connected to this world, that is, either in the realm of hell, hungry ghosts, animals, human beings, or heavenly beings. If the self is not a conditioned one, then it will not be reborn in any of the five realms."

"What does master Gotama mean by that?"

"As to rebirth, Vaccha, I declare it to be for what has fuel, not for what is without fuel.

"Just as, Vaccha, a fire with fuel blazes up, but not without fuel, even so, Vaccha, do I declare rebirth to be for what has fuel, not for what is without fuel."

"But, master Gotama, at the time when a flame, flung by the wind, goes a very long way, as to fuel what says the master Gotama about this?"

"At the time when a flame, Vaccha, flung by the wind, goes a very long way, I declare that flame to be supported by the wind. At that time, Vaccha, the wind is its fuel."

"But, master Gotama, at the time when a being lays aside this body and rises up again in another body, what does master Gotama declare to be the fuel for that?"

"At the time, Vaccha, when a being lays aside this body and rises up again in another body, for that I declare craving (*tanha*) to be the fuel. Indeed Vaccha, craving is on that occasion the fuel."

Vacchagotta the Wanderer felt these words keenly. He understood that all sentient beings who are unable to extinguish craving will reincarnate into this world of ignorance after they die; only a Buddha is an Unconditioned One because he has extinguished craving (*tanha*) and attained Nirvana. "Wonderful! Wonderful!" he said. Then he got up and went away.

Shakyamuni uses the metaphor of fire and fuel to explain the reappearance of existence to Vacchagotta.

Fire (life, the self) is dependent upon fuel (the body) to burn. When the fuel is gone the fire will become extinct. However, even after the fuel has been consumed, embers, kindling coals, remain. These coals, conditioned by craving, are another body (the continuation of other skandhas). These remaining embers, aroused by the winds of karma, seek a new source of fuel (a physical body) and then, igniting, begin a new fire.

The characteristics of this new fuel and new fire are determined by the nature of the craving and the form of the other skandhas that are its kindling embers, and by the winds of karma that arouse its reappearance.

The word *tanha* that Shakyamuni uses here is usually translated as craving. The original meaning of the word is to be thirsty. The descriptive characteristic that the Buddha is trying to communicate in this teaching is the intensity of the craving for water; he is trying to convey the extreme acuteness of desire and attachment.

The Buddha has used a figurative expression rather than a technical term to convey his concept. But when the Chinese translators went to codify this term they did it in a way that entirely misses the point. They originally chose the ideographs 'thirst' and 'love' to translate *tanha*, but gradually reduced this to the ideograph for 'love' alone.

Bun'yu Masutani has this to say about the matter:

> Gotama Buddha also uses the word *raga* to express craving. In his early sermons he often uses the word *tanha*, but he soon begins to use the term *raga* more frequently. The original meaning of *raga* can be 'red' or 'flame'. Gotama Buddha compares blazing desire to a red flame. The Chinese translators chose the ideograph for 'greed' to represent this term. Something is definitely lost in the translation...
> (*Bukkyo no shiso* [Buddhist Ideas], Kadokawa Shoten)

Similarly, when the Chinese translators decided to use the ideographs 'thirst-love' and then 'love' for *tanha*, a certain quality was erased from the Buddha's intended meaning.

Tanha is the thing that triggers rebirth and reincarnation. As such, the words 'thirst-love' and 'love' don't create the correct image of the mental mechanism that is at work here.

The word *tanha* (thirst) is an entirely appropriate expression when used in the context of a tropical country like India, because in that kind of environment, different from a temperate climate like Japan's, the lack of water is a seriously life-threatening condition that causes real fear and suffering.

It is difficult to capture in words that quality of the mental energy of a craving so acute and all consuming that it has the power to move a human being onward into their next lifetime.

"I put a curse on you that you will die. I promise you that this curse will live after me."

"May I be reborn forever until I finish this."

Consuming, one-pointed thoughts and attachments like these actually have the power to pull us forward into the next lifetime.

We should never forget that such an awesome power lurks inside each and every one of us.

Chapter 3

What Reincarnates?
The Brain and the Mind

What Reincarnates?

In the previous section I addressed the issue of why people reincarnate. I would now like to discuss the matter of what it is that actually does the reincarnating.

So what do you think it is?

At the end of the last chapter I introduced the Buddhist idea that *tanha* (mental craving) is the 'thing' that reincarnates. Or, at the very least, *tanha* is what induces reincarnation.

I imagine that this statement is quite bewildering to most people, especially because there is a general belief in contemporary society that the mind and the brain are the same thing. And if the mind and the brain are identical it follows that the human mind would perish along with the brain at the time of death. If the mind is reduced to nothing, then how can it reappear later on? If the above were true, reincarnation wouldn't make sense.

What is there besides 'the mind' (and the *tanha* it engenders) that could be the thing that reincarnates? It's pretty impossible to imagine it being anything else. But if the mind and the brain are the same thing then reincarnation couldn't happen.

Yet we know that it does.

So, are the brain and the mind identical?

The modern scientific establishment, particularly neurologists, favor the argument that the mind is simply a function of the physical brain.

How can we dispute this? Let us give it a try.

The Brain-Only Theory:
The Mind as a Function of the Brain

Professor Takeshi Yoro, an anatomist with the medical faculty of Tokyo University, tries to answer this question decisively in his book *Yuinoron* (Brain-Only Theory). He contends that the mind is solely a function of the brain. He uses clear logic to make the argument that the brain and the mind are one and the same thing.

Here is an excerpt from Dr. Yoro's work:

Is the Mind Generated by the Brain?

"The idea that the mind arises from the mass of physical matter we call the brain is a ridiculous notion. Isn't the mind something much more subtle and mysterious than that?"

In their simplest forms, the mind/body theories of philosophy arise from this basic question. Add to this the arguments of the theologians. They believe that the only beings who can even have a mind, or spirit, are man and God. This is an idea that is rooted in Christian theology, so it may not make intuitive sense to those of us from a different culture. We have a saying that "even an insect has a soul half its size." So we might not have such a hard time with the idea that the mind arises out of the brain. Some may believe it already. But it is still strange to think that something as abstract and non-material as the mind can

137

come from a lump of physical matter like the brain. And this is the essence of the question that has long occupied the imaginations of the non-scientific community.

Brain-only theory provides a simple answer to the question. It posits that the relationship between the mind and the brain is one of form (or structure) and function.

Let us examine the problem in concrete terms. "How does the brain, which is composed of physical matter, give rise to the mind? If you say that the mind is part of the brain, then why can't you find the mind when you take the brain apart? Where is it? Because the truth is you can't find the mind, no matter how hard you look, by dissecting the physical lump of matter we call the brain."

It is a common question, but there is a basic flaw in this conventional way of thinking. And how can we expect to come up with the correct answer if a question is not asked correctly in the first place? The following example should help to clarify the situation.

We know that the heart is the foundation of the circulatory system and that when the heart stops so does the circulation. But if we break down the cardiovascular system into its component parts, do we find the part that gives rise to the circulation? No. Circulation is not attributable to any one of the fundamental elements of the system—not the veins, nor the arteries, nor the heart. We can dissect the heart. We cannot dissect the circulation. The only dissection we can perform on the circulation is metaphorical, because the heart is the 'form' and circulation is the 'function.'

By inference, this example helps us to understand the apparently contradictory nature of the mind/brain connection. The brain definitely is a material substance. We can isolate it as a thing and examine it as such. We can measure how much it weighs. The mind, however, is the function of the brain that indicates the brain is operational. Circulation as a function of the material form of the heart can't be found in the heart, and the mind as a function of the material form of the brain can't be found in the brain. The systems are each of a piece, the names pertain to whether we are looking at the system from the perspective of form or of function. That's all there is to it.

If one believes that the mind is something different than the function of the brain it is also easy to panic when one can't find the mind when one dissects the brain. I suggest that this, too, is a mistake. It's true we can't find it, but this doesn't mean it is something other, in the same way that the circulation isn't other than the heart. Saying the mind can't be found in the brain supports the correct supposition that function can't be found in form.

This logical argument does not only apply to the mind, of course. But we make a big deal out of the specific function of the brain we call the 'mind' because we believe that the mind is something extraordinarily special.

Why do we make this *a priori* distinction between the brain as structure and mind as function? It is because our brain is constructed in a way that makes us incapable of not taking this point of view. This is how brain-only theorists would answer our original question. And it is not an evasion. One of the peculiarities of the human brain is that it is designed to discern this kind of a separation between the structure and function of the biological organs. This fact is immediately apparent when we examine the structure of the brain.

Dr. Yoro, as an anatomist, examines the functionality of the brain from various structural perspectives, and concludes:

In summary, I contend that the mind is ultimately nothing more than a function of the nervous system and that the brain is just one structural component of this system.

I have presented the above argument as a representative illustration of brain-only theory, the theory that claims the mind and the brain are one and the same thing.

Do We Have More Than One Mind?

So we see that there are some people who think the mind is one of the functions of the human brain, but there are also some neuro-anatomists who propose the opposite supposition, that the brain is one of the functions of the mind.

Dr. Atsushi Yamatori, an assistant professor of psycho-physiology at Kobe University Medical School, recounts two case histories that demonstrate amazing ways the brain can function in his book *No kara mita kokoro* (The Mind Viewed from the Brain).

He notes that "Geschwind and Sperry have developed the revolutionary hypothesis that there might be more than one mind."

Dr. Yamatori views the workings of the mind from the viewpoint of the brain, whereas Dr. Yoro views the functioning of the mind from the anatomical perspective.

Dr. Yamatori offers the published accounts of two case histories to support his position.

Both of the cases he cites concern changes that occurred in the relationship between linguistic and artistic ability in patients who suffered brain damage. The objective examination of this relationship would require a human subject whose proficiencies in speech and artistic ability were equally developed before the onset of brain damage, someone like a professional musician. The statistical probability of encountering someone like this is very low.

Dr. Yamatori recounts: "There was a doctor in the Soviet Union who had the rare opportunity of treating such a patient. His name was Dr. Luria, and he kept meticulous records of detailed information about the case. Let us look at what Dr. Luria found."

Composing Brilliant Music in Spite of Aphasia

There was a famous musician named Professor Shebalin who was elected Professor of the Moscow Conservatorie and directed a class of composition. Many well-known Russian composers were among his pupils. During the next few decades he composed a series of symphonies, and one of his operas was performed at the Moscow Bolshoi Theatre.

He suffered for many years from vascular hypertension. When he was 51 he sustained an acute disturbance of his cerebral circulation with a slight impairment of cutaneous sensibility in the right hand, accompanied by a paresis of the right side of the face and a severe disturbance of his speech. After some weeks these symptoms disappeared and the patient was able to return to his work.

For the next 6 years he worked actively as a composer and also as a Director of the Moscow Conservatoire. Then when he was 57 he had a second stroke. He suffered impaired speech and a light paralysis on his right side. This time he never recovered from the aphasia. He lived for another three and half years before he died of a heart attack.

He was under the medical care of Dr. Luria and his practice for these last 3 1/2 years.

Shebalin's aphasia was quite severe. He often made mistakes in phonemes and words. He would start to say something and then lose track of what he was saying and be unable to finish. He had trouble expressing himself. He wasn't always able to call up the correct word for the thing he was trying to represent and he lost the ability to name certain objects, even if he was shown a pictorial representation of it or the object itself. His comprehension was also severely damaged. Shebalin was frustrated by the fact that he had lost his ability to grasp the meaning of certain words, and would complain bitterly in simple language about his inability to understand their meaning.

The professor never recovered from his condition. As Luria noted, using more technical terminology, Shebalin continued to exhibit 'acute panlingual impediment accompanied by auditory type aphasia'.

Luria further reported that, in spite of his handicap, the professor continued to create new musical work. He kept producing his own compositions and continued to review and criticize the work of his many students. Moreover, the level of his own mastery did not seem to decrease as a result of his condition.

Dr. Luria has left us a record that attests to his patient's amazing dedication over that three-year period. Here is the list of the pieces that the professor wrote during that time:

Op. 51 (1959–1960): Sonata for violoncello and pianoforte, C-flat; in four parts. Performed by M.Rostropovich, S.Knuchevitsky and others.

Op. 52 (1960–1962): Three Choruses on Moldavian Motives (played by the Moldavian Capella).

Op. 53 (1960): The Eighth Quartette (played by the Borodin Quartette, Moscow; recorded).

Op. 54 (1960): My Fatherland (eight songs, awarded a prize).

Op. 55 (1961): The Land of Moldavia (three songs, performed by G. Vishnevskaya of the Bolshoi Theater).

Op. 56 (1962): The Fifth Symphony, C-flat; for orchestra, in four parts (performed by the Orchestra of the USSR; recorded).

Op. 57 (1963): To My Grandchildren; four choruses (in print).

Op. 58 (1963): The Ninth Quartette in three parts (recorded).

Op. 59 (1963): In the Middle of the Forest; seven choruses (performed by the Svechnikov Chorus; in print).

Op. 60 (1963): Sonatina G-flat in three parts (played by Kramskoi; in print).

What a remarkable output! The professor's determination to create new work certainly didn't suffer as a result of his handicap; if anything, it may have actually increased. And not only did he continue to produce work, it remained at a high level. In addition to winning awards and being recorded, the work was performed by leading musicians. This all testifies to its quality.

Luria includes statements by some of Shebalin's famous contemporaries that confirm his patient's achievements:

Shostakovitch says:

"Shebalin's *Fifth Symphony* is a brilliant creative work, filled with highest emotions, optimistic and full of life. This symphony composed during his illness is a creation of a great master."

Khrennikov says:

"We can only envy the brilliant creative activity of this outstanding man who, in spite of his illness, created the brilliant *Fifth Symphony* full of young feelings and wonderful melodies."

Let me present another remarkable case. This one concerns the relationship between the faculty of speech and visual artistic ability.

The ability to draw pictures, which only we have been given, is something that represents a vast difference between man and the other primates. The caves of Altamira and Cognac contain Stone Age paintings done 30,000 years ago that demonstrate a wonderful artistic sensibility, even when looked at from a contemporary perspective. In these images, the essential forms of the subjects have been clearly cognized and depicted using bold, abstract strokes. The legacy of graphic expression left to us in the darkness of these caves is a testament to the continuing intellectual power of *homo sapiens*.

What do we know about the cortical relationship between verbal ability and the power of such artistic expression?

A survey of the literature reveals an account of another rare case history that speaks specifically to this point. This case is found in an article by a French neurologist named Alajouanine entitled *Aphasia and Artistic Realization* that was published in 1948. The name of the patient was not disclosed at the time of publication but was made public later on, so I will take the liberty of noting it here. His name was François Dernier.

Painting Beautiful Pictures while Aphasic

In his time (the 1940s), Dernier typified the contemporary modern artist, and was known for his highly idiosyncratic work. According to Alajouanine's synopsis, his work contained brilliantly poetic depictions of the Normandy coast such as the sparkling beauty of the plant and marine life and the loveliness of the female inhabitants. Dernier was an accomplished poet and musician as well as a painter. Influences from his metier, the youthful exuberance of Baudelaire, and the exquisite musicality of Debussy could be felt in his work.

When he was 52 years old he was suddenly deprived of language after two short and transient aphasic spells. His spoken language was much impaired; paraphasia is striking, voluntary vocabulary finding much disturbed, but understanding remains quite good because mainly of an intuitive grasp of the general meaning of conversation... Intellectual impairment is not to be found. Although oral or written conversation became very difficult especially when concerned with the aesthetic problems in which he used to be interested one can easily realize that memory, judgment and taste are not at all impaired...

Artistic realization in our painter since his aphasia remains as perfect as before. According to connoisseurs, he has perhaps gained a more intense and acute expression...One cannot find since his language deterioration any mistake in form, expression or colour interpretation. There are no changes in the interpretation of sensorial data, no technical failure; neither is there any disturbance of thought. I am of the opinion that he lays emphasis on thematic characteristics with a poetical strength, in a completely unaltered manner, and that since his illness he has even accentuated the intensity and the sharpness of his artistic realization. Moreover, his activity and production have not slowed down...

This sort of example teaches us that the neurological structures that govern speech and those that govern artistic ability are functionally separate. Alajouanine comments: "It seems that our painter's artistic production goes on as if nothing had happened, and that in him the aphasic and the artist live together on two distinct planes..."

Dernier himself speaks about the difficulty of his predicament. "There are in me two men, the one who paints, who is normal while he is painting, and the other one who is lost in the mist, who does not stick to life... I am saying very poorly what I mean...There are inside me the one who grasps reality, life: there is the other one who is lost as regards abstract thinking. When I am painting I am outside my own life; my way of seeing things is even sharper than before; I find everything again; I am a whole man. Even my right hand that seems strange to me, I do not notice when I am painting. These are two men, the one who is grasped by reality to paint, the other one, the fool, who cannot manage words any more."

Dernier's own words are riveting. I believe they contain a valuable message.

Namely, his statements suggest the possibility that there is something other than the cerebral motor tract which perceives and creates beauty. And I would contend that that something is the 'mind'.

Dernier's neurological mechanisms of speech may have been impaired but he seems to have another mind that perceives and creates beauty, and this one clearly remained sound.

This example suggests that this mind is what controls the cerebral motor tract and moves it to paint pictures; that causes it to paint.

Which leads to the theory that the mind is the thing that perceives and creates beauty. It further suggests that the mind is a separate mechanism from that of the cerebral motor tract, that the mind controls the nerves and commands them to paint pictures.

The case of Professor Shebalin suggests the same conclusion.

Now, in response to our findings, the brain-only theorists would probably make a reductionist stab at our reasoning. They would say: "Along with everything else, the creative mind is just another product of the workings of the nervous system. It is just one aspect of the operation of the brain. That's just the way the brain is. There is no 'mind' that exists independently from the brain. The brain is the mind."

Period.

And yet we are forced to disagree.

I have shown that there are world-famous neurologists

who seem to agree with my line of thinking.

Before I introduce more on this topic, I would first like to make a few comments on my own relationship to neuroanatomy.

Mind/Body Theory—
Is the Mind Separate from the Brain?

A thought like this one has never even crossed my mind: "The idea that the mind arises from the mass of physical matter we call the brain is a ridiculous notion. Isn't the mind something much more subtle and mysterious than that?" It is just too simplistic.

I myself don't find it at all strange that the brain exhibits incredibly amazing and awe-inspiring characteristics because it is a part of this extraordinary human body, this aggregate of matter that functions with such unbelievable subtlety. After looking at it from various angles, we still can't easily conclude that the brain and the mind are the same thing. We have to continue to search for their real relationship.

Professor Yoro makes a valiant attempt to convince us that his theory about form and function is correct, but his argument denigrates the intelligence of his audience. There is no reason for him to go to such lengths.

Buddhism manages to resolve this issue in one short poem:

The mountain cherry trees of Yoshino
Bloom year after year
Yet chop down a tree
Where can you find the flowers?

The cherry tree is the form. The blossoming flowers are the function.

No matter how finely we chop up a tree, no matter how closely we dissect it, we will never find a profusion of flowers in glorious blossom inside there. But every year when springtime comes, the cherry trees boast branches heavily laden with blooms.

It didn't matter to me whether the brain is composed of physical matter or of non-matter. It was irrelevant to me whether the mind is a component of the brain or the other way around.

Either way, there is *something* that transmigrates.

I wanted to snow where this *something* is located.

It exists, so it has to be located somewhere.

I only wanted to pin down where that somewhere is.

And that is why I began, as a lay person, to study neurophysiology.

In Search of Powers that Go beyond the Functions of the Brain

My marked interest in the field of neuroanatomy began a long time ago, about forty years before I began to study the subject.

It is possible that I may be the first Buddhist leader, particularly in the esoteric tradition, who has undertaken such a serious examination of the field. I have written about this topic in a number of different books, including *Henshin no genri* (The Principle of Transformation), *Mikkyo: Chonoryoku no himitsu* (Esoteric Buddhism: The Secret of Paranormal Abilities), and *Kanno shiko* (Interbrain Thinking).

I didn't decide to tackle such difficult subject matter out of mere curiosity. I was driven to it by necessity.

There were two reasons for this need.

The first time I picked up a book on brain physiology was after I had begun the spiritual practice taught in Shingon Buddhism known as *Gumonjisomeiho*, or the Morning Star Meditation. This practice made me realize that I needed to understand the structure and functioning of the brain.

I had received transmission of this esoteric practice, one that is supposed to result in the ability to remember everything seen and heard, turning an ordinary person into a genius. I tried hard to follow the ritual manual exactly, but the only thing I noticed was an intensification of my ability to concentrate. So I decided to review the whole process again, and to look at each element of it very carefully. After examining it thoroughly, I couldn't see how it could turn an ordinary mind into one of a genius. Something was missing. It didn't have all the elements required for that sort of transformation.

At the same time, I knew that Kukai (Kobo Daishi) had practiced this meditation when he was young and that it was reputed to have engendered his legendary genius. I was even using the version of the ritual manual that he himself had formalized.

Maybe there were secrets hidden somewhere within the text of instructions. If there were I was determined to uncover them. And if I couldn't find any hidden secrets, if the system turned out to be flawed, then I figured I would have to come up with a new, more effective, version of the *Gumonjisomeiho*. So I started to study the anatomy of the brain. I was looking for clues that might help me solve this dilemma.

Looking back on it now, I see how my youthful bravado and tenacity helped me begin to achieve my goal, though it took the later study of kundalini yoga to finally grasp what I was looking for.

Knowledge of the brain was useful when I began the practice of kundalini yoga to develop my brain chakras. In fact, I never could have awakened my brain chakras through the practice of kundalini yoga if I didn't understand the physiology of the brain, no matter how hard I might have tried.

The second reason for studying the brain arose when I started to perform 'the 7 systems and 37 practices for attaining Buddhahood'. These practices made me realize that I needed an even deeper understanding of how the brain works.

The purpose of the Morning Star Meditation is to elevate the functioning of the brain. Specifically, it is supposed to improve one's memory. (Not just simple memory, however.)

But now I saw that in order to master the method of

attaining Buddhahood one had to develop powers that went beyond the brain's ordinary functions. These are powers that come from the awakening and perfecting of one's spirituality.

This realization left me with two burning questions:

Is spirituality one of the brain's functions?

And, if so, where is that function located?

There I was. On the one hand I was religiously performing 'the 7 systems and 37 practices for attaining Buddhahood', and, on the other, I was doggedly searching for a map of the inside of the brain.

The Crocodile, the Horse, and the Human Being that Coexist inside Our Brain

The writer who coined the term holonic science, Arthur Koestler, wrote a book entitled *Janus* in which he propounds that there is a fundamental and fatal flaw in the human brain. Koestler's reasoning plunged him into a great sense of despair, and he ended up taking his own life.

I believe the reason Koestler arrived at such an unhappy conclusion is because he insisted on examining the brain solely from the perspective of function. Anyone who examines the brain solely from the perspective of anatomy, from that of its neurological function, is bound to come up with a similar conclusion.

Arthur Koestler was a genius, but in his work on the human brain he never recognized any other functions than those of the brain itself. His mistaken conclusions are due to the fact that he only examined the brain in light of the mechanisms of its discrete parts.

He writes in *Janus*:

> The most striking indication of the pathology of our species is the contrast between its unique technological achievements and its equally unique incompetence in the conduct of its social affairs.

Man's predicament has turned our history into the history of war, and is now leading us down the path towards extinction...

> The most persistent sound which reverberates through man's history is the beating of war drums. Tribal wars, religious wars, civil wars, dynastic wars, national wars, revolutionary wars, clolonial wars, wars of conquest and of liberation, wars to prevent and to end all wars, follow each other in a chain of compulsive repetitiveness as far as man can remember his past, and there is every reason to believe that the chain will extend into the future...
>
> ...as the devices of nuclear warfare become more potent and easier to make, their spreading to young and immature as well as old and arrogant nations becomes inevitable, and global control of their manufacture impracticable. Within the fore-seeable future they will be made and stored in large quantities all over the globe among nations of all colours and ideologies, and the probability

that a spark which initiates the chain-reaction will be ignited sooner or later, deliberately or by accident, will increase accordingly, until, in the long run, it approaches certainty. One might compare the situation to a gathering of delinquent youths locked in a room full of inflammable material who are given a box of matches—with the pious warning not to use it.

How in the world did we ever get to such a dangerous place, one in which we are facing the potential destruction of our planet? Koestler claims, as per the following argument, that the reason for this mess is because there is something fundamentally wrong with the human brain. He bases his theory on the so-called Papez-MacLean theory of emotions:

The theory is based on the fundamental differences in anatomy and function between the archaic structures of the brain which man shares with the reptiles and lower mammals, and the specifically human neocortex, which evolution superimposed on them—without, however, ensuring adequate coordination. The result of this evolutionary blunder is an uneasy coexistence, frequently erupting in acute conflict, between the deep ancestral structures of the brain, mainly concerned with instinctive and emotional behaviour, and the neocortex which endowed man with language, logic and symbolic thought. MacLean has summed up the resulting state of affairs in a technical paper, but in an unusually picturesque way:

Man finds himself in the predicament that Nature has endowed him essentially with three brains which, despite great differences in structure, must function together and communicate with one another. The oldest of these brains is basically reptilian. The second has been inherited from the lower mammals, and the third is a late mammalian development, which...has made man peculiarly man. Speaking allegorically of these three brains within a brain, we might imagine that when the psychiatrist bids the patient to lie on the couch he is asking him to stretch out alongside a horse and a crocodile.

The 'reptilian' and 'paleo-mammalian' brains together form the so-called limbic system which, for the sake of simplicity, we may call the 'old brain', as opposed to the neocortex, the specifically human 'thinking cap'. But while the antediluvian structures at the very core of our brain, which control instincts, passions and biological drives, have been hardly touched by the nimble fingers of evolution, the neocortex of the hominids expanded in the last half a million years at an explosive speed which is without precedent in the history of evolution—so much so that some anatomists compared it to a tumorous growth.

This brain explosion in the second half of the

Pleistocene seems to have followed the type of exponential curve which has recently become so familiar to us... But explosions do not produce harmonious results. The result in this case seems to have been that the rapidly developing thinking cap, which endowed man with his reasoning powers, did not become properly integrated and coordinated with the ancient emotion-bound structures on which it was superimposed with such unprecedented speed. The neural pathways connecting neocortex with the archaic structures of the mid-brain are apparently inadequate.

Thus the brain explosion gave rise to a mentally unbalanced species in which old brain and new brain, emotion and intellect, faith and reason, were at loggerheads. On one side, the pale cast of rational thought, of logic suspended on a thin thread all too easily broken ; on the other, the raging fury of passionately held irrational beliefs, reflected in the holocausts of past and present history.

If neurophysiological evidence had not taught us the contrary, we would have expected it to reveal an evolutionary process which gradually transformed the primitive old brain into a more sophisticated instrument—as it transformed gill into lung, or the forelimb of the reptilian ancestor into the bird's wing, the flipper of the whale, the hand of man. But instead of *transforming* old brain into new, evolution *superimposed* a new superior structure on an old one with partly overlapping functions, and without providing the new brain with a clear-cut power of control over the old.

To put it crudely: evolution has left a few screws loose between the neocortex and the hypothalamus. MacLean has coined the term *schizophysiology* for this endemic shortcoming in the human nervous system. He defines it as

...a dichotomy in the function of the phylogenetically old and new cortex that might account for differences between emotional and intellectual behaviour. While our intellectual functions are carried on in the newest and most highly developed part of the brain, our affective behaviour continues to be dominated by a relatively crude and primitive system, by archaic structures in the brain whose fundamental pattern has undergone but little change in the whole course of evolution from mouse to man.

In summary, then, Koestler examines the human brain through its component structures and their functions, anatomically and neurophysiologically. He does not recognize the possibility of any mental function within the brain that might exist alongside of its component functions.

I'd like to excerpt a portion of my book *Kanno shiko* (Interbrain Thinking) that deals with Koestler's theory.

The 'Spiritual' Part of the Human Brain

The excerpt reproduced here recounts a dialogue I had with a well-known journalist and producer, the late S.K.

"Well now. Let's begin our discussion of today's issue. Here is what Arthur Koestler has to say." Mr. K. starts by quoting the following passage in *Janus*.

> *Homo sapiens* may be an aberrant biological species, an evolutionary misfit, afflicted by an endemic disorder...
>
> ...The evidence from man's past record and from contemporary brain-research both strongly suggest that at some point during the last explosive stages of the biological evolution of *homo sapiens* something went wrong; that there is a flaw, some potentially fatal engineering error built into our native equipment—more specifically, into the circuits of our nervous system—which would account for the streak of paranoia running through our history. This is the hideous but plausible hypothesis which any serious inquiry into man's condition has to face.

"So," Mr. K. began, "Koestler seems to be saying that, as a species, we are on the brink of extinction. Reverend Kiriyama, may I ask what you think about this? Do you agree with Koestler that the human being is a biological freak who has a fatal flaw in the design of his brain?"

"No, I don't believe that. I think that the way our brain is designed is close to perfection."

"In that case, do you think that we've somehow failed to evolve in accordance with the way we were designed?"

"Yes, I do. And I also agree with Koestler's inference that the failure occurred at an explosive point in our evolution. But I don't think there is a flaw in the basic design. I just think that somewhere during the course of evolution we got off track. I bring up this point in my book *Mikkyo: Chonoryoku no himitsu* (Esoteric Buddhism: The Secret of Paranormal Abilities)."

"Could you give us some concrete examples of what you mean?"

"I believe that the human brain has a spiritual component. This component is part of its original design. If that component had functioned the way it was supposed to, the human race would never have developed the streak of insanity that Koestler talks about. And, consequently, we never would have gotten ourselves into this predicament, one in which we are looking straight ahead at our own ruination. The spiritual component shut down at some point during the evolutionary process. This is why we have become a race of such 'great fools'."

"That is certainly a startling idea."

"But it's not just an idea. It's the truth."

"Where do you think this spiritual component is located?"

"It's located in the hyperthalamus of the diencephalon, or interbrain, which is in the innermost center of the cerebrum. The spiritual component is found in the deepest part of that structure. However, for this component to function, the nearby endocrine body, the pineal gland, has to be activated in a specific way."

"Is this an accepted view of neurophysiology?"

"No, it isn't. It is something that I discovered for myself through my own spiritual practice. It is a conclusion that I came to after gathering information from many sources: empirical evidence gained through the practice of the disciplines of Indian kundalini yoga and Tibetan Vajrayana Buddhism, as well as others. Neurophysiology hasn't come this far yet. But I found an interesting statement by the American endocrinologist J.D. Ratcliff. In *The Miracle of the Human Body*, Ratcliff says:

> We are almost on the verge of understanding the function of the pineal gland, which is a small cone-shaped gland located at the base of the brain. At this point, it is presumed that the pineal gland is a vestigial third eye that we have received from our primitive ancestors.

"Do you know about the third eye?" I asked Mr. K.

"A long time ago I read a book with a title that was something like that," he answered. "It was by some Englishman who had been practicing Vajrayana Buddhism with Tibetan lamas. He wrote about experiencing the opening of the third eye between his eyebrows and being able to see the fourth dimension and the spiritual world. The book was a best-seller. I don't remember much about what he said, but I know that I read it," he replied.

"Let me quote something I wrote in the chapter

'Hormones and the Third Eye':

> People may think that the idea of a third eye is totally fanciful and idiotic. But human beings used to have one. No, actually, we still do. We find evidence of it when we investigate the endocrine system, which controls the most essential functions of the human body.
>
> We find evidence not only that man used to possess a third eye, but it is also clear that it is not the 'vestigial' organ that Ratcliff would have us believe.
>
> I contend that, when properly activated, the third eye can still function in the here and now as an organ of sight. There is scientific proof to this effect.
>
> Before I go on to introduce the results of these experiments, I'd like to elaborate on the marvelous workings of the endocrine system..."

"So, Reverend, is this third eye the same thing as the spiritual component of the brain that you are talking about?"

"No, not exactly. They have a close relationship, but they are not identical. The third eye, as Ratcliff says, is the pineal gland. The spiritual component of the brain is located in the deeper stratum of the hyperthalamus."

"And how are these two different?"

"Briefly, the third eye is able to perceive various phenomena of the spiritual dimension. It is an organ that possesses the faculty of observation. The hyperthalamus is the 'field' that activates and controls this faculty. In other words, they have a relationship similar to the one between the conventional eyes and the brain."

"I see."

"In my book I go on to explain, from the viewpoints of neuroanatomy, endocrinology, and enzyme pharmacology, why I think the spiritual 'field' is located in the hyperthalamus.

"Human spirituality manifests when the hyperthalamus acts in connection with the third eye. Ultimately this leads to the attainment of Godhead or Buddhahood.

"The interbrain, the locus of the 'spiritual' field, lies in between the neo-cortex with its reason and logic and the limbic system that is the seat of the instincts. It is what provides us with balance. Our problem is that our fields of spirituality have been shut down."

"Hmmm."

"However, there have always been certain people throughout history who understood this. Shakyamuni Buddha was one of them. The Buddha perfected a system to reactivate this field of spirituality. We call this system 'the method of attaining Buddhahood'. Early esoteric Buddhism inherited this system."

"Why do you use the term early esoteric Buddhism?"

"In later esoteric Buddhism the original system that Shakyamuni taught was formalized in accordance with Mahayana principles. During this process it was transformed into something else entirely."

"That makes sense."

"But we can still see traces of this early esoteric Buddhism in certain statues and paintings of the Buddha.

In many esoteric Buddhist statues the Buddha has a third eye."

"You mean the eye that we see between the eyebrows?"

"Yes, that's the one. Maheshvara (*Daijizaiten*, Jp.) is one of these representative esoteric Buddhist deities. He is said to be one of the eight protectors of the world. Maheshvara is always depicted with three eyes, one of them a third eye between his eyebrows.

"Human beings have two visible eyes. One of them is connected to the limbic brain and one is connected to the neo-cortex. The two eyes work as a pair, and enable us to see the phenomenological (material) world. But then we have another one connected to the hyperthalamus of the diencephalon. This is what we call the third eye. It is the one that can see the spiritual dimension."

"So are you saying, Reverend, that the spiritual field ceased to function at the same time that the third eye became vestigial?"

"Well, yes, but it's more like the third eye stopped working because the spiritual field was closed off and ceased functioning. That's when the eye became vestigial. And that's because they have this close interdependent relationship..."

"Hmmm."

Mr. K thought for a moment.

"But...," he said, looking skeptical, "How did human beings lose this spiritual field to begin with? It couldn't be simple atrophy. Our mental activity has advanced and evolved so rapidly since pre-historic times that I can't believe it could be due to some kind of degeneration."

"Do you want to know the reason?" I asked him.
He nodded.

The Disappearance of the Third Eye

I answered: "There is a major reason, of course, why the third eye was shut down. The 'field' of spirituality naturally aspires to a higher sphere, one that tries to control, even to oppose, the materialistic desires and instincts that belong to the mental domain. People might expect this function to belong to the neo-cortex, but it doesn't.

"The intellect of the neo-cortical system attempts to comprehend the nature of God or of Buddha in an analytical fashion, whereas the field of spirituality has the inclination to unify with God directly. It has the will to become Buddha. Spirituality is not a function of the neo-cortical system.

"The intellect produced in the neo-cortex, to quote Dr. Tokizane, aims at 'living better' and 'living higher'. It pursues these objectives by engaging in purposeful activity. Looking at the results of all this activity, we find philosophy (morality and ethics) in the mental realm and science (and technology) in the material. Or, in other words, the goal of 'living better' has given rise to science and technology, and that of 'living higher' has produced philosophy and ethics. But philosophy and ethics seem to have reached a dead end. They are not helping us solve the problems we are facing right now, although they are broadcasting plenty of warning signals.

"Meanwhile, the neo-cortical goal of 'living better' has

turned into the pursuit of 'more convenience' and 'more speed'. Just think about it. Contemporary society is the civilization of the neo-cortex, and our material civilization is the creation of that same body. The goals of contemporary society could even be summed up by the slogan 'easier and faster'. All the business enterprises on the face of the planet are frantically working to accomplish these goals. And even when our neo-cortex becomes uncomfortably aware of the way it is backing us into a corner it is still helpless to stop. That's because the neo-cortex itself long ago inhibited the function of the interbrain and opposed the 'field' of spirituality, thus robbing us of the power to resist following its dictates."

"How could that happen?"

"This is a phenomenon that we ordinarily associate with the cerebral evolution of animals. As an animal progresses up the evolutionary ladder its neo-cortex develops in a way that acts to gradually push the archicortex further into the base strata of the cerebral hemisphere, forcing the old cortex into the interior of the cerebral hemisphere. This is the accepted opinion of cerebral physiology. The same thing happened in the human brain.

"The neo-cortex justifies its domination over the interbrain as being in the interests of the evolution and advancement of humankind, as contributing to the cause of peace and prosperity. Coming up with this kind of rationalization is a special forte of the neo-cortex. As I said before, 'the "field" of spirituality naturally aspires to a higher sphere, one that tries to control, even to oppose, the materialistic desires and instincts that belong to the mental domain.' In other words, spirituality puts the brakes on the material culture produced by the neo-cortex. Depending on one's point of view, one could even say that spirituality is the enemy of the neo-cortex. The neo-cortex reacts to this oppression by trying to disempower the 'field' of spirituality. And all of our instincts (the limbic brain) join in the battle on the side of the neo-cortex. This seems to be our 'karma' as human beings.

"This is the fundamental reason why our so-called intellect has the tendency to treat the whole notion of spirituality and spiritual objects with such hostility and, even today, to dismiss spirituality as superstition. Self-styled proprietors of great intelligence have been known to bare their fangs and attack when they even hear the word 'spirituality'."

"I see, I see." Mr. K laughed out loud at this. "So at what point in human history did the neo-cortex gain domination over the interbrain?"

The Age when Intelligence (the Neo-cortical Brain) and Spirituality (the Interbrain) Flourished Simultaneously

I answered his question by asking one of my own.

"Mr. K, you made the comment before that 'our mental activity has advanced and evolved rapidly since pre-historic times.' Are you sure about this?"

"Pardon me?"

"It seems to me that, in fact, we haven't made any progress at all since ancient times. For all I know, we may even be regressing."

"What do you mean?"

"I believe that our spiritual culture reached its apex thousands of years ago, and that nothing truly new has been produced since that time. We're just following in the footsteps of those who led the way. The peak of intellectual culture was achieved before the Christian era. This is especially true for wisdom cultures that are based in spirituality."

"Hmmmmm."

"For example, the classics, which one might view as the prime examples of human intellectual achievement, can largely be classified into one of three major groups: Chinese, Greek, and Indian. I don't have any of these texts with me for reference. But, in broad strokes, we know that the authors of the Chinese classics, beginning with Confucius in the 5th century B.C. and continuing on with Mencius, Mozi, Zhuangzi, Xunzi, and Sima Qian, all lived before the birth of Jesus Christ.

"In Greece, Homer wrote the *Iliad* and the *Odyssey* in the 8th century B.C., Aesop was born in the 7th century B.C., and the mathematician Pythagoras, the philosopher Heraclitus, and the dramatists Aeschylus and Sophocles all lived in the 5th century B.C. The renowned Socrates, Plato, and finally Aristotle were active in the 4th century B.C. These are the individuals who laid the foundation of later European intellectual culture, and the intellectual products of contemporary Western civilization are unimaginable without them.

"I don't think we have created anything in the interim that surpasses the original contributions of the ancients."

"Interesting."

"The Indian classics date back even earlier. The *Rig Veda* was composed 3,000 years ago, that's 10 centuries before the birth of Christ. Brahmanism coalesced in the 8th century B.C., and the *Upanishads* were formulated in the 7th century B.C. Shakyamuni Buddha was born in 556 B.C."

"Hmmm."

"In the Middle East, Moses led the exodus out of Egypt 13 centuries before the common era, the prophet Isaiah appeared in the 8th, and Zoroaster established his religion in the 7th, the same century in which the prophet Jeremiah was active. Then Christ's birth signaled the dawn of the first millennium."

"......." Mr. K. nodded silently.

"Doesn't it seem," I continued, "like all these flowers bloomed at the same time? Isn't it possible that the classical period was the summit of our spiritual civilization so far?

"Here is another way to look at it: During the golden age, intellectuality (or the neo-cortex) and spirituality (or the interbrain) flourished simultaneously. After that time, the neo-cortex made rapid advances. In Greece, the neo-cortex gave us the birth of philosophy and that enabled the development of the sciences. This development has resulted in our ability to harness the energy of the sun and to land a man on the moon.

"And sometime during this process of rapid, explosive growth, the neo-cortex shut down the third eye and the field of spirituality in the hyperthalamus, allowing what we call science to satisfy our materialistic desires. It almost seems that, for some reason, the field of spirituality had to be shut down in order for this to happen.

"And then the resulting imbalance in the brain went on to manifest as an imbalance within the species. The term *homo sapiens* means 'wise man' but this imbalance fills us with so many contradictions that we can also be called 'great fools'. It is affecting the balance of the entire planet, as if the whole world were an expression of the human brain or the brain that which shapes the world. It is no wonder that Koestler speaks about our species' 'unique technological achievements and its equally unique incompetence in the conduct of its social affairs' and 'our streak of insanity'. But the imbalance in the world that has been created by this biological disparity is not something that will continue forever..."

It is my firm contention that the human interbrain possesses a field of spirituality.

This field of spirituality turns a human being into the 'lord of creation' who is able to manifest and recognize divinity such as God or the Buddha.

I conclude, in short, that the interbrain is where the human mind is located.

And yet even though I am sure about this, I am still a layperson. You might accuse me of being arbitrary and biased.

I will try to counter this by introducing the work of Dr. Wilder Penfield, a renowned neurosurgeon who propounds a similar theory. Please take a look at the following.

Penfield's *The Mystery of the Mind*

I conducted my intensive study of the brain in a highly random, disorganized manner. I read a world of books, surveying the breadth and depth of the copious amount of professional literature. I didn't read these books in any systematic fashion, just read whatever I could get my hands on. In the process, my own sort of system emerged.

During this time I ran across many excellent theories that electrified me, but nothing, before or since, has amazed or thrilled me as much as the work of Dr. Wilder Penfield. The extent to which I quoted him in *Mikkyo: Chonoryoku no himitsu* (Esoteric Buddhism: The Secret of Paranormal Abilities), a book I wrote over 20 years ago, attests to my enthusiasm.

But as a layperson my praise can only go so far, so I will rely on the words of Dr. William Feindel, the Director of the Montreal Neurological Institute and Professor of Neurosurgery at McGill University. Here is some of what Dr. Feindel has to say in his introduction to Dr. Penfield's book *The Mystery of the Mind*:

> Among the various groups of research workers and physicians concerned with the enormous task of exploring the "nerve-cell jungle" of the human brain, neurosurgeons alone have the unusual opportunity and privilege of being able to observe directly the living brain, and to map out its responses to stimulation, in the course of bringing

therapeutic relief to their patients. And for many reasons, Dr. Wilder Penfield's distinguished contributions to this special field have been recognized as unique by his neurosurgical and scientific colleagues. During his lifelong devotion to the care of patients with focal epilepsy, he has catalogued a great body of information that has provided further insight for us into "the physiology of the mind." (This phrase, Dr. Penfield notes, was used in 1872 by John Hughlings Jackson, the British neurologist who introduced the concept of increasingly complex levels of function in the brain.) He was able to do this from a substantial background of scientific preparation. As a student in the laboratory of Sir Charles Sherrington at Oxford, he had the chance to develop meticulous surgical technique and systematic recording of observations, which he further refined for use in the operating room and clinic...

In another stage of scientific study, Dr. Penfield visited the Spanish histological school of Ramon y Cajal in Madrid. Cajal was then the acknowledged "maestro" of the microscopic study of the brain...

From Cajal and his brilliant pupil Rio-Hortega, Dr. Penfield learned techniques to examine the microscopic nature of brain scars, which are sometimes associated with epilepsy. He further pursued this problem with Professor Otfried Foerster in Breslau, a neurologist turned neurosurgeon, and one of the few at that time who had persevered in the treatment of epilepsy by surgical removal of the brain scar.

Then in 1934, Dr. Penfield and his associates at McGill University established the Montreal Neurological Institute. This combined the facilities of a special hospital for nervous diseases, with the resources of brain research laboratories. Here, over a period of some thirty or more years of intense work, he directed scientific and surgical teams toward solutions of many unanswered questions about the brain, such as the mechanism of epilepsy, the learning of language, and how the brain remembers.

One example of these investigations might be given here, since it is a key point in any discussion of mind and brain. In 1952, Dr. Penfield and I were working side by side in the operating room observing the responses of patients to gentle electrical current applied to the temporal lobe. We became aware that in some patients, it was possible to produce, artificially, a curious state of automatism. During this, the patient became unaware, mouthed inappropriate comments—one patient was heard to say "time and space seem occupied"—made semi-purposeful movements, and, strangest of all, later had no memory of all this. We had come earlier to recognize, as did Hughlings Jackson years before, that similar behavior was a hallmark of a particular kind of epileptic seizure. We were now able to identify that this could be initiated from a deep part of the temporal lobe, from an amazingly local region, a small almond-shaped island of nerve cells, called the amygdala (from the Greek word for almond). It was evident that the nerve-cell discharge, set off by the stimulation, produced a train of complex events in the brain that seemed to isolate the patient's awareness and memory-recording from his motor and sensory activities. In fact, it seemed apparent that the patient had "lost his mind" in the real sense of the meaning of this ancient word...

(These experiments in automatism would later form the important foundation of the theory on the differentiation between the brain and the mind. —Kiriyama)

This present book brings to us a distillation of the scientific writings of Dr. Penfield and his gradually evolving views of functional localization and interaction within the human brain. In addition, he has now moved on to a much deeper discussion of the brain-mind question...

Dr. Penfield's present analysis derives from his accumulation of direct observations on the human brain in conscious patients. In that important sense, it transcends significantly all earlier studies; either those of physiologists, who argued from a basis of experimental animal findings, or those of neurologists, psychologists, or psychiatrists, whose views were related to interpretations of the external motor and emotional behavior of patients with focal brain disorders. Many readers will recognize that the research findings summarized here by Dr.

Penfield are fundamental to our understanding of memory, learning, language, and behavior. As one of his final conclusions, Dr. Penfield supports the proposition that there is something that character- izes mind as distinct from physical brain.[i]

The Highest Brain-Mechanism

Dr. Penfield himself says:

> The automatic mechanisms of the brain inter- act with, and may be separated from, the brain's machinery-for-the-mind...[ii]

Penfield bases his explanation of the existence of the 'highest brain-mechanism' on his observations of the symp- toms of automatism. When a patient suffers the loss of the highest brain mechanism, the faculty of purposeful, planned behavior can no longer be observed.

> And so it is that the mechanism in the higher brain-stem, whose action is indispensable to the very existence of consciousness, can be put out of action selectively! This converts the individual into a *mindless automation...*

i. Wilder Penfield, *The Mystery of the Mind*, pp. xxv–xxix
ii. Ibid., p. 37

The human automation, which replaces the man when the highest brain-mechanism is inactivated, is a thing without the capacity to make completely new decisions. It is a thing without the capacity to form new memory records and a thing without that indefinable attribute, a sense of humor. The automaton is incapable of thrilling to the beauty of a sunset or of experiencing contentment, happiness, love, compassion. These, like all awarenesses, are functions of the mind. The automaton is a thing that makes use of the reflexes and the skills, inborn and acquired, that are housed in the computer. At times it may have a plan that will serve it in place of a purpose for a few minutes. This automatic coordinator that is ever active within each of us, seems to be the most amazing of all biological computers.

By listening to patients as they describe an experiential flashback, one can understand the complexity and efficiency of the reflex coordinating and integrative action of the brain. In it, the automatic computer and the highest brain-mechanism play interactive roles, selectively inhibitory and purposeful.

Does this explain the action of the mind? Can reflex action in the end, account for it? After years of studying the merging mechanisms within the human brain, my own answer is "no." Mind comes into action and goes out of action with the highest brain-mechanism, it is true. But the mind has energy. The form of that energy is different from

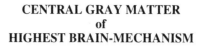

CENTRAL GRAY MATTER
of
HIGHEST BRAIN-MECHANISM

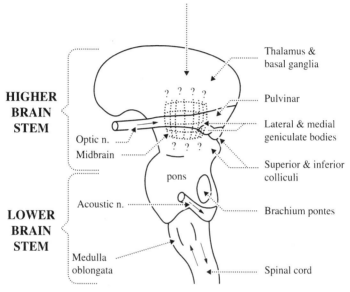

The Highest Brain-Mechanism

The site of the central gray matter of this brain-mechanism, the normal action of which constitutes the physical basis of the mind, is shown by the dotted lines. The question marks indicate only that the detailed anatomical circuits involved are yet to be established, not that there is any doubt about the general position of this area in which cellular inactivation produces unconsciousness. Such inactivation may be brought about variously by pressure, trauma, hemorrhage, and local epileptic discharge; it occurs normally in sleep. (Drawing by Eleanor Sweezey.)

that of neuronal potentials that travel the axone pathways.

In concluding this section, Penfield says:

> I assume that the mind directs, and the mind-mechanism executes. It carries the message. As Hippocrates expressed it so long ago, "the brain is messenger" to consciousness. Or, as one might express it now, the brain's highest mechanism is "messenger" between the mind and the other mechanisms of the brain.[iii]

The Relationship between Consciousness and the Brain: A Dramatic Case Study

Dr. Penfield offers the following dramatic example in the chapter of his book entitled "The Relationship between Consciousness and the Brain: A Case Study":

> Consciousness can be present whenever the highest brain-mechanism is normally active, even though adjacent parts of the brain are inactivated by some abnormal influence. A patient, whom I was called upon to see in Moscow under dramatic circumstances in 1962, illustrated the fact that conscious understanding may be present when

---

iii. Penfield, op. cit., pp. 46–48

motor control has been lost completely, or almost completely, and when the brain is not capable of making a permanent record of the stream of consciousness.

The patient was the brilliant physicist, Lev Landau. Only intensive nursing had kept him alive during six weeks of complete unconsciousness following a head injury in an automobile crash. On my first examination of the patient, I agreed that he was completely unconscious. I then recommended a minor diagnostic operation (ventriculography). His limbs were paralyzed; his eyes were open but apparently unseeing. Next morning, when I entered his room to examine him again, I was accompanied by his wife. She preceded me and, sitting down at the bedside, she talked to him, telling him that I had suggested to the Soviet surgeons that he should have a brain operation. As I stood silent, watching over her head, I became aware of a startling change in the patient. He lay unmoving still, as on the previous night. But his eyes, which had been deviated from each other then, were focused now in a normal manner. He seemed to be looking at her. He appeared to hear, and see, and to understand speech! How could this be? She came to the end of her explanation and was silent. His eyes then moved upward to focus quite normally on me. I moved my head from side to side. The eyes followed me. No doubt about it! Then they swung apart again and he appeared, as he had the night before, to be unconscious.

It was clear that the man had returned to consciousness. He had been able to hear, see, understand speech, but not to speak. He could not move, except to focus and turn his eyes briefly. Perhaps I should explain that he and his wife had been separated for a time. It was our talk of possible operation that had led to her being summoned to Moscow and to the hospital. She was seeing him that morning for the first time since the accident.

It was thrilling to realize what had happened. He had been roused by her presence and probably understood her message. Evidently the hemispheres above the higher brain-stem, with their speech and visual and auditory mechanisms, had not been injured. The to-and-fro exchange between brain-stem and cortex was free, but when he sent neuronal messages out to the peripheral motor nuclei in the lower brain-stem and spinal cord, none could pass the block at the level of the hemorrhage in the midbrain. None, that is, except those to the eye movement center, which is highest of all the peripheral centers for motor control. If he was conscious, he must have sent down many other messages that would normally have flashed outward to the muscles. His wife was an appealingly handsome woman. His mind may well have sent a message intended to cause his hand to take hers. But his hand lay motionless.

However that may be, I went back to the other doctors and we decided that no operation was necessary. I had seen the first sure sign of recovery. He was transferred at once from the outlying hospital, in which he had been nursed so magnificently, to the Moscow Neurosurgical Institute, where he would have the great advantage of supervision by Professor B. G. Egorov. Physiotherapy was begun at once, and I learned later that there was slow but continuous and progressive recovery from that day onward.

For the first six weeks after the accident, Landau's fellow physicists, most of them his disciples, had joined the nurses and doctors in their gallant effort to keep the patient breathing and capable of recovery if that should prove possible. This man, who had already been awarded the Lenin Prize for his contributions to physics, was given the Nobel Prize during his convalescence. He and his wife were happy together and she was with him on the special occasion of his acceptance of the award...

...I learned still later that Landau did continue to improve in the year that followed, and was able to tutor his son in preparing for his university entrance examinations. Great recognition came to this man whose mathematical genius has been likened to that of Einstein. His countrymen rejoiced at his recovery but the "depression" returned to him. Perhaps he realized that his brain could no longer serve him as it had.[iv]

---

iv. Penfield, op. cit., pp. 46–71

Comprehensibility

Dr. Penfield writes in the last chapter of his book, titled "Comprehensibility":

Taken either way, the nature of the mind presents the fundamental problem, perhaps the most difficult and most important of all problems. For myself, after a professional lifetime spent in trying to discover how the brain accounts for the mind, it comes as a surprise now to discover, during this final examination of the evidence, that the dualist hypothesis seems the more reasonable of the two possible explanations.

Since every man must adopt for himself, without the help of science, his way of life and his personal religion, I have long had my own private beliefs. What a thrill it is, then, to discover that the scientist, too, can legitimately believe in the existence of the spirit!

In the remainder of this chapter I shall at times speak less as a physiologist and more as a physician who, in addition to his addiction to science, is concerned about his patients, his family, and himself. But I shall do my best to take critical judgement with me each time I step "outside the boundaries of natural science."

Possibly the scientist and the physician could

add something by stepping outside the laboratory and the consulting room to reconsider these strangely gifted human beings about us. Where did the mind—call it the spirit if you like—come from? Who can say? It exists. The mind is attached to the action of a certain mechanism within the brain. A mind has been thus attached in the case of every human being for many thousands of generations, and there seems to be significant evidence of heredity in the mind's character from one generation to the next and the next. But at present, one can only say simply and without explanation, "the mind is born..."

...Here, as I approach the end of this study, is a further suggestion from the physician's point of view. It is an observation relevant to any inquiry into the nature of man's being, and in conformity with the proposition that the mind has a separate existence. It might even be taken as an argument for the feasibility and the possibility of immortality!

"What becomes of the mind after death?"

That question brings up the other question so often asked: "Can the mind communicate directly with other minds?" As far as any clearly proven scientific conclusion goes, the answer to the second question is "no." The mind can communicate only through its brain-mechanisms. Certainly it does so most often through the mechanism of speech. Nonetheless, since the exact nature of the mind is a mystery and the source of its energy has yet to be identified, no scientist is in a position to say that direct communication between one active mind and another cannot occur during life. He may say that unassailable evidence of it has not yet been brought forward.

Direct communication between the mind of man and the mind of God is quite another matter. The argument, in favor of this, lies in the claim, made by so many men for so long a time that they have received guidance and revelation from some power beyond themselves through the medium of prayer. I see no reason to doubt this evidence, nor any means of submitting it to scientific proof.

Indeed, no scientist, by virtue of his science, has the right to pass judgement on the faiths by which men live and die. We can only set out the data about the brain, and present the physiological hypotheses that are relevant to what the mind does.

Now we must return, however reluctantly, to the first question: when death at last blows out the candle that was life, the mind seems to vanish, as in sleep. I said "seems." What can one really conclude? What is the reasonable hypothesis in regard to this matter, considering the physiological evidence? Only this: the brain has not explained the mind fully. The mind of man seems to derive its energy, perhaps in altered form, from the highest brain-mechanism during his waking hours. In the daily routine of a man's life, communication with other minds is carried out indirectly through the mechanisms of the brain. If this is so, it is clear that, in order to survive after death, the mind *must* establish a connection with a source of energy other than that of the brain. If not, the mind must disappear forever as surely as the brain and the body die and turn to dust. If, however, during life, when brain and mind are awake, direct communication is sometimes established with the minds of other men or with the mind of God, then it is clear that energy from without can reach a man's mind. In that case, it is not unreasonable for him to hope that after death the mind may waken to another source of energy.

I mean that if the active mind of a man does communicate with other active minds, even on rare occasions, it could do so only by the transfer of some form of energy from mind to mind directly. Likewise, if the mind of man communicates with the mind of God directly, that also suggests that energy, in some form, passes from spirit to spirit. It is obvious that science can make no statement at present in regard to the question of man's existence after death, although every thoughtful man must ask that question. But, when the nature of the energy that activates the mind is discovered (as I believe it will be), the time may yet come when scientists will be able to make a valid approach to a study of the nature of a spirit other than that of man.[v]

---

v. Penfield, op. cit., pp. 85–89

This great scientist, after repeated experiments into virgin territory, concludes:

> It is an observation relevant to any inquiry into the nature of man's being, and in conformity with the proposition that the mind has a separate existence. It might even be taken as an argument for the feasibility and the possibility of immortality!

I have the deepest admiration for Dr. Penfield's bravery. Here is a scientist of his stature saying:

> What a thrill it is, then, to discover that the scientist, too, can legitimately believe in the existence of the spirit!

I can't praise his courage enough.

The more a person is entrenched in his or her own discipline, the more afraid he or she is to venture outside the boundaries of known territory. He becomes too concerned with damaging his reputation, and finds it safer to speak out from positions in the worlds in which he is familiar and has established credentials.

This is particularly true for scientists. Most people believe that for a scientist to speak about spirit is to risk professional suicide. And so scientists tend to keep their mouths shut.

I have a great feeling of admiration for Dr. Penfield's achievements, but I have an even greater sense of respect for his courage.

It Is Not the Brain that Commits Crimes, But the Mind

I've heard there is a criminology research institute in the United States that preserves the brains of dangerous felons by pickling them in formaldehyde.

That may be so, but I'm afraid that no amount of research into the brains of criminals will produce any substantial findings.

This is because the brain isn't what makes human beings commit evil deeds. It's the mind.

The brain is not what commits crimes. The mind is what commits crimes.

Of course, if a certain part of the brain becomes morbid, it may cause the commission of a crime. But in that case we don't say the person is a criminal, we say he is a psychopath.

If there was a region in the brain that did cause people to commit crimes and do bad things, then we could just go ahead and surgically remove it. Similar to when we remove the scar tissue from the brains of epileptics. If that was possible, then all we'd have to do is figure out how to augment the parts of the brain that are responsible for doing good deeds. Maybe we could create human beings that were almost like God, or Buddha. But, unfortunately, this isn't going to happen. There isn't any one part of the brain that turns a person into a criminal. The brain is not what commits crimes; the mind is.

If we make an analogy to a computer, we can say that the brain is like the hardware and the mind is like the software that runs it.

When a person is born into this world they acquire a new body, and, naturally, when they get a new body it has a new brain attached to it. But the mind that goes into the new brain comes from the last lifetime (or from many previous lifetimes, or from countless generations of lifetimes) and already possesses a long and old stream of experience. Various factors such as habitual tendencies, likes and dislikes, dispositions, and temperaments that a person has possessed over this long expanse of time are etched into his or her inborn character. Buddhism refers to these individual elements as habitual energies (*vasana*).

Each and Every Person Is a Reincarnate

The mind is not a memory machine. The brain is the mechanism that performs that function. The mind is the mechanism that preserves the seeds from the past. It's like Dr. Penfield says:

> The mind is attached to the action of a certain mechanism within the brain. A mind has been thus attached in the case of every human being for many thousands of generations, and there seems to be significant evidence of heredity in the mind's character from one generation to the next and the next.

Some psychologists would say that it is impossible to change a person's character. If it can be changed then it isn't character. I would say this is because a person's character is made up of these past seeds from his or her former lives. That is why it is useless to try to educate or reform the brain.

The brain acts upon commands from the mind; the brain can't give orders to the mind. This is the way our neurological system is structured. And we are all born into this world with everything from our pasts etched into our minds. In this way, then, we can say that every human being is a reincarnated existence.

The Emergence of Past Life Habits and Talents

Now, I just said that the mind is not a memory machine. But even though the mind doesn't record memory the same way that the brain does, there are many instances where habitual energy from a past life manifests as the propensities, habits, thoughts, and talents, etc., of the present lifetime.

To cite some well-known examples, Heinrich Schliemann, the archaeologist who excavated Troy, declared when he was only 8 years old that he was going to find that city. Jean François Champollion, the founder of Egyptology, expressed a profound interest in that country from the time he was little. According to his recollections of later years, he decided that he was going to decipher Egyptian hieroglyphics before he was 12. And Michael Ventris, the linguist who eventually decoded Mycenaean Linear B, was 7 years old when he bought his first book in German about Egyptian hieroglyphics and began his study of the subject. He made a vow to decipher the script when he was only 14.

The mathematical genius Evariste Galois was so incredibly precocious that nobody believed he could be for real. If we don't take past life memory and experience into consideration, it's hard to account for the sudden appearance of this kind of brilliance.

In general, great composers show a profound affinity and aptitude for music from the time they are very young. In some cases this early interest can be attributed to the influence of their parents or other family members. Bach, Mozart, Beethoven, Brahms, and Elgar, for example, all had fathers who were musicians.

On the other hand, Dvorak's father was a meat processor, Delius's father was an industrialist, Mendelssohn's father was a banker, and Handel's father was a barber/surgeon. We know for a fact that Handel's father was vehemently opposed to his son becoming a musician, and that young Handel defied him from the time he was a child. There is no evidence that any of these composers inherited anything musical from their ancestors.

Ian Stevenson notes in his book *Children Who Remember Previous Lives* that "many subjects have expressed in their play the vocation of the previous personality." He then offers some interesting examples:

Wijanama Kithsiri regularly opened a play shop when he came home from school; and Parmod Sharma's mother grumbled that he had squandered a year in playing at having a tea and biscuit shop. Both of these subjects remembered lives in families of shopkeepers. Ma Tin Aung Myo (whose case I summarized in chapter 4) and Bajrang B. Saxena played at being soldiers when they were young children; they remembered the lives of soldiers. Vias Rajpal, who remembered the life of a doctor, used to pretend to take the temperatures of his playmates and listen to their chests. Daniel Jirdi, who recalled the life of an automobile mechanic, would lie under his family's sofa and make believe that he was under a car that he was repairing. Lalitha Abeyawardena, who remembered the life of a schoolteacher, assembled her playmates in the form of a class and used a stick to point to an imaginary blackboard in front of which she would play at teaching.

Judith Krishna, who as a young child remembered the life of a sweepress (in India), gathered twigs, which she put together in the form of a broom (of the type used by sweepers), and with this she would sweep out her family's compound. I mentioned earlier another young Indian girl, Swaran Lata, who remembered the life of a sweepress; she had particularly dirty habits, but she cleaned up the excrement of the younger children of the family with seeming pleasure. Both these last two subjects were daughters of middle-class parents in whose families the behavior of a sweeper was as unexpected as it was unwelcome.

Subjects of these cases may also express in play an addictive habit of the person whose life they remembered. For example, I have known two children who remembered the lives of alcoholics and in their play gave amusing demonstrations of how a drunken person staggers around and collapses. One of these children was Sujith Lakmal Jayaratne, whom I have already mentioned in connection with the phobias he had of trucks and policeman.

Other subjects have relived in play how the previous personality died. Ramez Shams, who remembered a life that ended in suicide (by shooting), used to enact the motion of shooting himself; another child, Maung Win Aung, who recalled a suicidal death by hanging, had the habit of playing with a rope around his neck in a seeming enactment of hanging himself. Three other subjects who remembered previous lives that ended in suicidal drowning used to play at drowning.[vi]

I have encountered similarly disturbing examples. I know a number of young people who are inveterate shoplifters, for instance. They were all habitual thieves in their former lives.

They all happen to come from upper-middle-class families who give them whatever they need, including

---

vi. Stevenson, op. cit., p. 183

allowances, but they still steal anyway. I know about these cases because their parents couldn't deal with them anymore and came to me for consultations. That's when I clairvoyantly looked into their pasts to figure out what was going on.

When I liberate the spirit of the former thieves, the present-day kleptomania stops completely. It is as though it never happened.

I know of one girl who, though still very young, kept getting sexually involved with men. Her behavior was pathological and painful to watch; she was just picking her partners at random. When asked about it she confessed that she wasn't in love with these men but she was helpless to stop herself from going with anybody who approached her. I investigated her past spiritually and found out that she had been a prostitute in a former lifetime.

When I liberated the spirit of her former self, her sexual acting-out ceased. This was a tragic story but at least she didn't come down with anything horrible like aids.

We always need to suspect some kind of past sexual abnormality in cases of unrestrained sexual behavior.

Also, an inordinate preoccupation with sex in young children is often a sign of reincarnate influence. The habitual energy from past marriages is emerging. Adult sexual complexes are also often rooted in past lives.

The actions of past lifetimes cast their shadows into our present lifetimes in ways that are often unexpected and sometimes shocking.

Chapter 4

Reincarnation
and the Afterworld

A Chronicle of Reincarnation

How does the actual process of transmigration and rebirth work?

In truth, I find that the process is different for each person.

However, I also recognize that there are certain fixed principles underlying the way reincarnation occurs. Let us now turn our attention to them.

I'd like to begin by introducing a remarkably detailed historical document which describes a case of reincarnation that occurred in Japan in the mid-nineteenth century.

Many tales of reincarnation have come down to us through the ages, but most of them are not credible. They tend to be based on hearsay and to contain faulty information such as incomplete or mistaken names of people and places.

But the following account has survived in the form of an official document, a written record that was made by an administrative agent for his feudal lord. It reports the details of a strange and important event that occurred in the lord's domain. All in all, the account is so complete in terms of story and particulars that it sounds very plausible.

This record of reincarnation was preserved by Lafcadio Hearn in his volume of essays *Gleanings in Buddha-fields*. I reprint it here.

The Rebirth of Katsugoro

I

The following is not a story,—at least it is not one of my stories. It is only the translation of an old Japanese document—or rather series of documents—very much signed and sealed, and dating back to the early part of the present century. My friend Amenomori, who is always seeking rare Japanese and Chinese MSS., and seems to have some preternatural power for discovering them, found this one in the library of Count Sasaki in Tokyo. Thinking it to be a curious thing, he obtained kindly permission to have a copy of it made for me; and from that copy the translation was done. I am responsible for nothing beyond a few notes appended to the text.

Although the beginning will probably prove dry reading, I presume to advise the perusal of the whole translation from first to last, because it suggests many things besides the possibility of remembering former births. It will be found to reflect something of the feudal Japan passed away, and something of the old-time faith,—not the higher Buddhism, but what is incomparably more difficult for any Occidental to obtain a glimpse of: the common ideas of the people concerning preexistence and rebirth. And in view of this fact, the exactness of the official investigations, and the credibility of the evidence accepted, necessarily become questions of minor importance.

II

1.—Copy of the Report of Tamon Dempachiro.

The case of Katsugoro, nine years old, second son of Genzo, a farmer on my estate, dwelling in the Village called Nakano-mura in the District called Tamagori in the Province of Musashi.

Some time during the autumn of last year, the above-mentioned Katsugoro, the son of Genzo, told to his elder sister the story of his previous existence and of his rebirth. But as it seemed to be only the fancy of a child, she gave little heed to it. Afterwards, however, when Katsugoro had told her the same story over and over again, she began to think that it was a strange thing, and she told her parents about it.

During the twelfth month of the past year, Genzo himself questioned Katsugoro about the matter, whereupon Katsugoro declared,—

That he had been in his former existence the son of a certain Kyubei, a farmer of Hodokubo-mura, which is a village within the jurisdiction of the Lord Komiya, in the district called Tamagori, in the province of Musashi;—

That he, Katsugoro, the son of Kyubei, had died of smallpox at the age of six years,—and

That he had been reborn thereafter into the family of the Genzo before-mentioned.

Though this seemed unbelievable, the boy

repeated all the circumstances of his story with so much exactness and apparent certainty, that the Headman and the elders of the village made a formal investigation of the case. As the news of this event soon spread, it was heard by the family of a certain Hanshiro, living in the village called Hodokubo-mura; and Hanshiro then came to the house of the Genzo aforesaid, a farmer belonging to my estate, and found that everything was true which the boy had said about the personal appearance and the facial characteristics of his former parents, and about the aspect of the house which had been his home in his previous birth. Katsugoro was then taken to the house of Hanshiro in Hodokubo-mura; and the people there said that he looked very much like their Tozo, who had died a number of years before, at the age of six. Since then the two families have been visiting each other at intervals. The people of other neighboring villages seem to have heard of the matter; and now persons come daily from various places to see Katsugoro.

A deposition regarding the above facts having been made before me by persons dwelling on my estate, I summoned the man Genzo to my house, and there examined him. His answers to my questions did not contradict the statements before-mentioned made by other parties.

Occasionally in the world some rumor of such a matter as this spreads among the people.

Indeed, it is hard to believe such things. But I beg to make report of the present case, hoping the same will reach your august ear,—so that I may not be charged with negligence.

[Signed] Tamon Dempachiro

The Fourth Month and the Sixth Year of Bunsei [1823].

2.—Copy of the Letter written by Kazunawo to Teikin, Priest of Sengakuji.

I have been favored with the accompanying copy of the report of Tamon Dempachiro by Shiga Hyoemon Sama, who brought it to me; and I take great pleasure in sending it to you. I think that it might be well for you to preserve it, together with the writing from Kwanzan Sama, which you kindly showed me the other day.

[Signed] Kazunawo

The twenty-first day of the Sixth Month. [No other date.]

3.—Copy of the Letter of Matsudaira Kwanzan [Daimyo] to the Priest Teikin of the Temple called Sengakuji.

I herewith enclose and send you the account of the rebirth of Katsugoro. I have written it in the popular style, thinking that it might have a good effect in helping to silence those who do not believe in the doctrines of the Buddha. As a literary work it is, of course, a wretched thing. I send it to you supposing that it could only amuse you from that point of view. But as for the relation itself, it is without mistake; for I myself heard it from the grandmother of Katsugoro. When you have read it, please return it to me.

[Signed]   Kwanzan

Twentieth day. [No date.]

[Copy.]
Relation of the Rebirth of Katsugoro.
4.—(Introductory Note by the Priest Teikin.)

This is the account of a true fact; for it has been written by Matsudaira Kwanzan Sama, who himself went [*to Nakano-mura*] on the twenty-second day of the third month of this year for the special purpose of inquiring about the matter. After having obtained a glimpse of Katsugoro, he questioned the boy's grandmother as to every particular; and he wrote down her answers exactly as they were given.

Afterwards, the said Kwanzan Sama condescended to honor this temple with a visit on the fourteenth day of this fourth month, and with his own august lips told me about his visit to the family of the aforesaid Katsugoro. Furthermore, he vouchsafed me the favor of permitting me to read the before-mentioned writing, on the twentieth day of this same month. And, availing myself of the privilege, I immediately made a copy of this writing.

[Signed]   Teikin So   Facsimile of the priest's *kaki-han*, or private sign-manual, made with the brush.

Sengaku-ji

The twenty-first day of the Fourth Month of the Sixth Year of Bunsei [1823].

[Copy.]

5.—[Names of the Members of the two Families concerned.]

[Family of Genzo.]

Katsugoro.—Born the 10th day of the 10th month of the twelfth year of Bunkwa [1815]. Nine years old this sixth year of Bunsei [1823].[1] Second son of Genzo, a farmer living in Tanitsuiri in Nakano-mura, district of Tamagori, province of Musashi.—Estate of Tamon Dempachiro, whose yashiki is in the street called Shichikencho, Nedzu, Yedo.—Jurisdiction of Yusuki.

Genzo.—Father of Katsugoro. Family name, Koyada. Forty-nine years old this sixth year of Bunsei. Being poor, he occupies himself with the making of baskets, which he sells in Yedo. The name of the inn at which he lodges while in Yedo is Sagamiya, kept by one Kihei, in Bakuro-cho.

Sei.—Wife of Genzo and mother of Katsugoro. Thirty-nine years old this sixth year of Bunsei. Daughter of Murata Kichitaro, samurai,—once an archer in the service of the Lord of Owari. When

---

1. The Western reader is requested to bear in mind that the year in which a Japanese child is born is counted always as one year in the reckoning of age.

Sei was twelve years old she was a maid-servant, it is said, in the house of Honda Dainoshin Dono. When she was thirteen years old, her father, Kichitaro was dismissed forever for a certain cause from the service of the Lord of Owari, and he became a *ronin*.[2] He died at the age of seventy-five, on the twenty-fifth day of the fourth month of the fourth year of Bunkwa [1807]. His grave is in the cemetery of the temple called Eirin-ji, of the Zen sect, in the village of Shimo-Yusuki.

Tsuya.—Grandmother of Katsugoro. Seventy-two years old this sixth year of Bunsei. When young she served as maid in the household of Matsudaira Oki-no-Kami Dono [*Daimyo*].

Fusa.—Elder sister of Katsugoro. Fifteen years old this year.

Otojiro.—Elder brother of Katsugoro. Fourteen years old this year.

Tsune.—Younger sister of Katsugoro. Four years old this year.

[Family of Hanshiro.]
Tozo.—Died at the age of six in Hodokubo-mura, in the district called Tamagori in the prov-

---

2. Lit.: "A wave-man,"—a wandering samurai without a lord. The *ronin* were generally a desperate and very dangerous class; but there were some fine characters among them.

ince of Musashi. Estate of Nakane Uyemon, whose yashiki is in the street Atarashi-bashi-dori, Shitaya, Yedo. Jurisdiction of Komiya.—[Tozo] was born in the second year of Bunkwa [1805], and died at about the fourth hour of the day [*10 o'clock in the morning*] on the fourth day of the second month of the seventh year of Bunkwa [1810]. The sickness of which he died was smallpox. Buried in the graveyard on the hill above the village before-mentioned,— Hodokubo-mura.— Parochial temple: Iwoji in Misawa-mura. Sect: Zen-shu. Last year the fifth year of Bunsei [1822], the *jiu-san kwaiki*[3] was said for Tozo.

Hanshiro.—Stepfather of Tozo. Family name: Suzaki. Fifty years old this sixth year of Bunsei.

Shidzu.—Mother of Tozo. Forty-nine years old this sixth year of Bunsei.

Kyubei (afterwards Togoro).—Real father of Tozo. Original name, Kyubei, afterwards changed to Togoro. Died at the age of forty-eight, in the sixth year of Bunkwa [1809], when Tozo was five years old. To replace him, Hanshiro became an *iri-muko*.[4]

---

3. The Buddhist services for the dead are celebrated at regular intervals, increasing successively in length, until the time of one hundred years after death. The *jiu-san kwaiki* is the service for the thirteenth year after death. By "thirteenth" in the context the reader must understand that the year in which the death took place is counted for one year.
4. The second husband, by adoption, of a daughter who lives with her own parents.

Children: Two boys and two girls.—These are Hanshiro's children by the mother of Tozo.

6.—[Copy of the Account written in Popular Style by Matsudaira Kwanzan Dono, Daimyo.]

Some time in the eleventh month of the past year, when Katsugoro was playing in the rice field with his elder sister, Fusa, he asked her,—

"Elder Sister, where did you come from before you were born into your household?"

Fusa answered him:—

"How can I know what happened to me before I was born?"

Katsugoro looked surprised and exclaimed:

"Then *you* cannot remember anything that happened before you were born?"

"Do you remember?" asked Fusa.

"Indeed I do," replied Katsugoro. "I used to be the son of Kyubei San of Hodokubo, and my name was then Tozo—do you not know all that?"

"Ah!" said Fusa, "I shall tell father and mother about it."

But Katsugoro at once began to cry, and said:
—

"Please do not tell!—it would not be good to tell father and mother."

Fusa made answer, after a little while:—

"Well, this time I shall not tell. But the next time that you do anything naughty, then I will tell."

After that day whenever a dispute arose between the two, the sister would threaten the brother, saying, "Very well, then—I shall tell that thing to father and mother." At these words the boy would always yield to his sister. This happened many times; and the parents one day overheard Fusa making her threat. Thinking Katsugoro must have been doing something wrong, they desired to know what the matter was, and Fusa, being questioned, told them the truth. Then Genzo and his wife, and Tsuya, the grandmother of Katsugoro, thought it a very strange thing. They called Katsugoro, therefore; and tried, first by coaxing, and then by threatening, to make him tell what he had meant by those words.

After hesitation, Katsugoro said:—"I will tell you everything. I used to be the son of Kyubei San of Hodokubo, and the name of my mother then was O-Shidzu San. When I was five years old, Kyubei San died; and there came in his place a man called Hanshiro San, who loved me very much. But in the following year, when I was six years old, I died of smallpox. In the third year after that I entered mother's honorable womb, and was born again."

The parents and the grandmother of the boy wondered greatly at hearing this; and they decided to make all possible inquiry as to the man called Hanshiro of Hodokubo. But as they all had to work very hard every day to earn a living, and so could spare but little time for any other matter, they could not at once carry out their intention.

Now Sei, the mother of Katsugoro, had nightly to suckle her little daughter Tsune, who was four years old;[5]—and Katsugoro therefore slept with his grandmother, Tsuya. Sometimes he used to talk to her in bed; and one night when he was in a very confiding mood, she persuaded him to tell her what happened at the time when he had died. Then he said:—"Until I was four years old I used to remember everything; but since then I have become more and more forgetful; and now I forget many, many things. But I still remember that I died of smallpox; I remember that I was put into a jar;[6] I remember that I was buried on a hill. There was a hole made in the ground; and the people let the jar drop into that hole. It fell *pon!*— I remember that sound well. Then somehow I returned to the house, and I stopped on my own pillow there.[7] In a short time some old man,— looking like a grandfather—came and took me

5. Children in Japan, among the poorer classes, are not weaned until an age much later than what is considered the proper age for weaning children in Western countries. But "four years old" in this text may mean considerably less, than three by Western reckoning.

6. From very ancient time in Japan it has been the custom to bury the dead in large jars,—usually of red earthenware,—called *Kame*. Such jars are still used, although a large proportion of the dead are buried in wooden coffins of a form unknown in the Occident.

7. The idea expressed is not that of lying down with the pillow under the head, but of hovering about the pillow, or resting upon it as an insect might do. The bodiless spirit is usually said to rest upon the roof of the home. The apparition of the aged man referred to in the next sentence seems a thought of Shinto rather than of Buddhism.

away. I do not know who or what he was. As I walked I went through empty air as if flying. I remember it was neither night nor day as we went: it was always like sunset-time. I did not feel either warm or cold or hungry. We went very far, I think; but still I could hear always, faintly, the voices of people talking at home; and the sound of the *Nembutsu*[8] being said for me. I remember also that when the people at home set offerings of hot *botamochi*[9] before the household shrine [*butsudan*], I inhaled the vapor of the offerings....Grandmother, never forget to offer warm food to the honorable dead [*Hotoke Sama*], and do not forget to give to priests—I am sure it is very good to do these things.[10]... After that, I only remember that the old man led me by some roundabout way to this place—I remember we passed the road beyond the village. Then we came here, and he pointed to this house, and said to me:—'Now you must be reborn,—for it is three years since you died. You are to be reborn in that house. The person who will become your grandmother is very kind; so it will be well for you to be conceived and born there.' After saying this, the old man went away. I remained a little time under the kaki-tree before

---

8. The repetition of the Buddhist invocation *Namu Amida Butsu!* is thus named. The *nembutsu* is repeated by many Buddhist sects besides the sect of Amida proper,—the Shinshu.

9. *Botamochi*, a kind of sugared rice-cake.

10. Such advice is a commonplace in Japanese Buddhist literature. By *Hotoke Sama* here the boy means, not the Buddhas proper, but the spirits of the dead, hopefully termed Buddhas by those who loved them,—much as in the West we sometimes speak of our dead as "angels."

the entrance of this house. Then I was going to enter when I heard talking inside: some one said that because father was now earning so little, mother would have to go to service in Yedo. I thought, "I will not go into that house;" and I stopped three days in the garden. On the third day it was decided that, after all, mother would not have to go to Yedo. The same night I passed into the house through a knot-hole in the sliding-shutters;—and after that I stayed for three days beside the *kamado*.[11] Then I entered mother's honorable womb.[12]... I remember that I was born without any pain at all,—Grandmother, you may tell this to father and mother, but please never tell it to anybody else."

The grandmother told Genzo and his wife what Katsugoro had related to her; and after that the boy was not afraid to speak freely with his parents on the subject of his former existence, and would often say to them: "I want to go to Hodokubo. Please let me make a visit to the tomb of Kyubei San." Genzo thought that Katsugoro, being a strange child, would probably die before long, and that it might therefore be better to make

11. The cooking-place in a Japanese kitchen. Sometimes the word is translated "kitchen-range," but the *kamado* is something very different from a Western kitchen-range.

12. Here I think it better to omit a couple of sentences in the original rather too plain for Western taste, yet not without interest. The meaning of the omitted passages is only that even in the womb the child acted with consideration, and according to the rules of filial piety.

inquiry at once as to whether there really was a man in Hodokubo called Hanshiro. But he did not wish to make the inquiry himself, because for a man to do so [*under such circumstances?*] would seem inconsiderate or forward. Therefore, instead of going himself to Hodokubo, he asked his mother Tsuya, on the twentieth day of the first month of this year, to take her grandson there.

Tsuya went with Katsugoro to Hodokubo; and when they entered the village she pointed to the nearer dwellings, and asked the boy, "Which house is it?—is it this house or that one?" "No," answered Katsugoro,—"it is further on—much further,"—and he hurried before her. Reaching a certain dwelling at last, he cried, "This is the house!"—and ran in, without waiting for his grandmother. Tsuya followed him in, and asked the people there what was the name of the owner of the house. "Hanshiro," one of them answered. She asked the name of Hanshiro's wife. "Shidzu," was the reply. Then she asked whether there had ever been a son called Tozo born in that house. "Yes," was the answer; "but that boy died thirteen years ago, when he was six years old."

Then for the first time Tsuya was convinced that Katsugoro had spoken the truth; and she could not help shedding tears. She related to the people of the house all that Katsugoro had told her about his remembrance of his former birth. Then Hanshiro and his wife wondered greatly. They caressed Katsugoro and wept; and they remarked that he was much handsomer now than he had been as Tozo before dying at the age of six. In the mean time, Katsugoro was looking all about; and seeing the roof of a tobacco shop opposite to the house of Hanshiro, he pointed to it, and said:—"That used not to be there." And he also said,—"The tree yonder used not to be there." All this was true. So from the minds of Hanshiro and his wife every doubt departed [*ga wo orishi*].

On the same day Tsuya and Katsugoro returned to Tanitsuiri, Nakano-mura. Afterwards Genzo sent his son several times to Hanshiro's house, and allowed him to visit the tomb of Kyubei his real father in his previous existence.

Sometimes Katsugoro says:—"I am a *Nono-Sama*:[13] therefore please be kind to me." Sometimes he also says to his grandmother:—"I think I shall die when I am sixteen; but, as Ontake Sama[14] has taught us, dying is not a matter to be afraid

---

13. *Nono-San* (or *Sama*) is the child-word for the Spirits of the dead, for the Buddhas, and for the Shinto Gods,—Kami. *Nono-San wo ogamu*,—"to pray to the Nono-San," is the child-phrase for praying to the gods. The spirits of the ancestors become Nono-San,— *Kami*,—according to Shinto thought.

14. The reference here to Ontake Sama has a particular interest, but will need some considerable explanation.

Ontake, or Mitake, is the name of a celebrated holy peak in the province of Shinano—a great resort for pilgrims. During the Tokugawa Shogunate, a priest called Isshin, of the Risshu Buddhists, made a pilgrimage to that mountain. Returning to his native place (Sakamoto-cho, Shitaya, Yedo), he began to preach certain new doctrines, and to make for himself a reputation as a miracle-worker, by virtue of powers said to have been gained during his pilgrimage to Ontake. The Shogunate considered him

of." When his parents ask him, "Would you not like to become a priest?" he answers, "I would rather not be a priest."

The village people do not call him Katsugoro any more; they have nicknamed him "Hodokubo-

---

a dangerous person, and banished him to the island of Hachijo, where he remained for some years. Afterwards he was allowed to return to Yedo, and there to preach his new faith,—to which he gave the name of Azuma-kyo. It was Buddhist teaching in a Shinto disguise,—the deities especially adored by its followers being Okuni-nushi and Sukuna-hikona as Buddhist avatars. In the prayer of the sect called Kaibyaku-Norito it is said:—"The divine nature is immovable (*fudo*); yet it moves. It is formless, yet manifests itself in forms. This is the Incomprehensible Divine Body. In Heaven and Earth it is called Kami; in all things it is called Spirit; in Man it is called Mind....From this only reality came the heavens, the four oceans, the great whole of the three thousand universes;—from the One Mind emanate three thousands of great thousands of forms."...

In the eleventh year of Bunkwa (1814) a man called Shimoyama Osuke, originally an oil-merchant in Heiyemoncho, Asakusa, Yedo, organized, on the basis of Isshin's teaching, a religious association named Tomoye-Ko. It flourished until the overthrow of the Shogunate, when a law was issued forbidding the teaching of mixed doctrines, and the blending of Shinto with Buddhist religion. Shimoyama Osuke then applied for permission to establish a new Shinto sect, under the name of Mitake-Kyo,— popularly called Ontake-Kyo; and the permission was given in the sixth year of Meiji [1873]. Osuke then remodeled the Buddhist sutra *Fudo Kyo* into a Shinto prayer-book, under the title, Shinto-Fudo-Norito. The sect still flourishes; and one of its chief temples is situated about a mile from my present residence in Tokyo.

"Ontake San" (or "Sama") is a popular name given to the deities adored by this sect. It really means the Deity dwelling on the peak Mitake, or Ontake. But the name is also sometimes applied to the high-priest of the sect, who is supposed to be oracularly inspired by the deity of Ontake, and to make revelations of truth through the power of the divinity. In the mouth of the boy Katsugoro "Ontake Sama" means the high-priest of that time [1823], almost certainly Osuke himself,—then chief of the Tomoye-kyo.

Kozo" (the Acolyte of Hodokubo).[15] When any one visits the house to see him, he becomes shy at once, and runs to hide himself in the inner apartments. So it is not possible to have any direct conversation with him. I have written down this account exactly as his grandmother gave it to me.

I asked whether Genzo, his wife, or Tsuya, could any of them remember having done any virtuous deeds. Genzo and his wife said that they had never done anything especially virtuous; but that Tsuya, the grandmother, had always been in the habit of repeating the *Nembutsu* every morning and evening, and that she never failed to give two *mon*[16] to any priest or pilgrim who came to the door. But excepting these small matters, she never had done anything which could be called a particularly virtuous act.

(— *This is the End of the Relation of the Rebirth of Katsugoro.*)

Isn't this a most interesting story?

---

15. *Kozo* is the name given to a Buddhist acolyte, or a youth studying for the priesthood. But it is also given to errand-boys and little boy-servants sometimes,—perhaps because in former days the heads of little boys were shaved. I think that the meaning in this text is "acolyte."

16. In that time the name of the smallest of coins = 1/10 of 1 cent. It was about the same as that now called *rin*, a copper with a square hole in the middle and bearing Chinese characters.

The Rebirth of Consciousness:
The Tibetan Book of the Dead

The *Bardo Thodol* (or *The Tibetan Book of the Dead*) is an esoteric text of Tibetan Buddhism that presents a detailed description of the realms one encounters after death and the process of reincarnation that one goes through.

I have found that there is an enormous variation in what actually happens to people after they die. This variation seems to depend on how much information they have about the process before they go through it. So the situation that a modern man or woman finds themselves in after they die is very different than that of an old-time Tibetan who received a lifetime of teachings about death from his or her lama.

Traditional Tibetans were more concerned with attaining peace in the afterworld than finding happiness in the here and now. That is because they knew the kind of terror they would experience when they died if they weren't prepared for the transition. They also knew that any happiness they might achieve on earth was fleeting compared to the lengthy period of fear and miserable despair they might have to endure when life was over.

Today most people have the simplistic notion that they only exist for this one lifetime and that they become nothing when they die.

The fact is that most of us don't know anything about it at all. The awful result of this ignorance is that we are totally unprepared to die and when we do it sends us into a state of overwhelming panic.

Tibetan people are given extensive knowledge about what is going to happen to them when they die and how to handle it. This enables them to go through the process of death calmly, without fear.

In contemporary society, however, we are given absolutely no knowledge about how to deal with the actual process of dying. The only resource we have to guide us through this terrifying time is our own reason. But when we die our ability to reason tends to disappear somewhere over the horizon. The profound changes that death brings are so unexpected that we become hysterical. Our response is antithetical to the measured reaction of someone who has been trained in what to expect. It's no wonder that modern man finds himself in a very different situation when he dies than in a scenario like the one described in *The Tibetan Book of the Dead*.

Here is some of what *The Tibetan Book of the Dead* has to say about reincarnation and the afterworld. I will add supplementary comments where I think they may be helpful.

The Tibetan Book of the Dead tells us that when a person dies his or her consciousness becomes absent. Then three and a half days later the person's consciousness abruptly returns. This is one of the points where I find a difference between what is stated in this text and actual experience. I have found that there is a great variation in when consciousness returns. Some people's consciousness returns soon after they stop breathing whereas other people's consciousness may not return for months.

I should note here that 'consciousness returning'

doesn't mean 'coming back to life'. The body remains dead; only consciousness revives.

The Sanskrit term for this stage of existence is *manomayakaya*, meaning 'mental body'. The individual manifests in a 'body' that is composed solely of consciousness, not flesh and blood.

The inherent state of awareness that belongs to this 'mental body' is of a relatively clear nature. However, if a person meets death in a state of intense suffering and vengefulness, these negative emotions are the mental elements that form the ensuing 'mental body'. They will act to cloud consciousness in a way that will impede the person's ability to realize that he or she is dead. When this happens, the dead person actually exists as an aggregate of these intense, negative feelings of pain and vengefulness. (And, in this form, projects a strong negative energy onto the people surrounding him or her.)

After a certain amount of time, however, clear light consciousness returns even to a being who has been clouded in this way.

The return of clear consciousness is a sign that the person has entered the intermediate state of existence that the Tibetans call the Bardo.

The Realm of the Bardo

Buddhism teaches that all sentient beings who possess

consciousness are born and die in a cyclic progression of birth and death, a process of transmigration, or flux, that has four modes of existence:

1. The mode of the moment of birth into a new existence
2. The mode of the span of time between birth and death
3. The mode of the moment of death
4. The mode of the intermediate span of time between death and birth into a new existence

This fourth mode of intermediate existence is what the Tibetans mean by the word *bardo*. In Sanskrit this is known as the *antarabhava*. And in Chinese it is referred to by terms that may be translated as 'the intermediate shadow' and 'the intermediate aggregate'.

This intermediate state has five different appellations, each of which refers to a specific characteristic of the being who exists there:

1. *Manomayakaya* = The being has a body that is made out of consciousness rather than flesh and blood.
2. *Sambhavaishin* = The being is desperately searching for his or her next incarnation.
3. *Gandharva* = The being lives on aroma essences of food and is inordinately fond of carnal pleasure.
4. *Antarabhava* = The being exists in the intermediate state between death and rebirth.
5. *Sambhava* = The being is nearing rebirth.

When a dead person enters the realm of the bardo he gradually gains a clear perception of his surroundings. This is when he realizes that he is dead. It comes as quite a shock.

The dead person cries out to his relatives and loved ones who he sees right there in front of him.

"Here I am! Stop grieving for me. Look, I'm over here!"

But his loved ones can't hear him, no matter how hard he yells. He can see them from where he is, but they can't see him. He can hear them wailing his name in grief, but his responses don't reach them, even when he shouts at the top of his lungs. This makes him feel unbearably frustrated and depressed.

Then three types of otherworldly phenomena appear. The dead person experiences completely unfamiliar sounds, colors, and rays of light. His fear, trembling, and astonishment cause him to faint. He comes back to consciousness. This can happen a number of times.

The dead person now feels an overwhelming desire to get back into his own body again. If his body is still lying there, he will try to re-enter it nine times in succession. If the body has already been cremated, the dead person will wander aimlessly around the urn that contains his remains, crying mournfully for himself.

Along with his desperation at not being able to re-enter his body, he is overcome by all the painful emotions and agonized thoughts he suffered when alive. He can't stand his feelings of regret and resentment. If he has a grudge against someone, he wants to go to that person and lash into him or her.

The Book of the Dead says:

> The living relatives may—by way of dedication for the benefit of the deceased—be sacrificing

many animals, and performing religious ceremonies, and giving alms. Thou, because of thy
vision not being purified, mayst be inclined to
grow very angry at their actions and bring about,
at this moment, thy birth in Hell: whatever those
left behind thee may be doing, act thou so that no
angry thought can arise in thee, and meditate
upon love for them.

Furthermore, even if thou feelest attached to
the worldly goods thou hast left behind, or,
because of seeing such worldly goods of thine in
the possession of other people and being enjoyed
by them, thou shouldst feel attached to them
through weakness, or feel angry with thy succes-
sors, that feeling will affect the psychological
moment in such a way that, even though thou
wert destined to be born on higher and happier
places, thou wilt be obliged to be born in Hell, or
in the world of *pretas* [or unhappy ghosts]. On the
other hand, even if thou art attached to worldly
goods left behind, thou wilt not be able to possess
them, and they will be of no use to thee. Therefore, abandon weakness and attachment for them;
cast them away wholly; renounce them from thy
heart. No matter who may be enjoying thy worldly
goods, have no feeling of miserliness, but be
prepared to renounce them willingly.

This admonition applies not only to material possessions. One needs to cast aside all of one's negative, resent-
ful feelings as well.

Unfortunately, this is the time that one is most vulnerable to one's negative feelings and the least able to control or dismiss them. When one is in this disembodied state, the entrenched feelings of vengeful hatefulness and remorse one has within oneself will take over. They will encompass one, swirling around mercilessly like an unending, raging storm. Certain feelings like those of attachment to possessions and anger may subside fairly easily, but feelings like true rage and resentment can be very difficult to silence. When these deep feelings continue unabated they will eventually turn the dead person into one of the negative disembodied spirits I have been referring to in this book, and many people get locked into this state for a very long period of time.

Wandering 'Mental Bodies'

The dead begin to wander.
The Tibetan Book of the Dead says:

O nobly-born, the possessor of that sort of body will see places [familiarly known on the earth-plane] and relatives [there] as one seeth another in dreams.

Thou seest thy relatives and connexions and speakest to them, but receivest no reply. Then, seeing them and thy family weeping, thou thinkest, 'I am dead! What shall I do?' and feelest great misery, just like a fish cast out [of water] on red-hot embers. Such misery thou wilt be experiencing at present. But feeling miserable will avail thee nothing now. If thou hast a divine *guru*, pray to him. Pray to the Tutelary Deity, the Compassionate One. Even though thou feelest attachment for thy relatives and connexions, it will do thee no good. So be not attached. Pray to the Compassionate Lord; thou shalt have nought of sorrow, or of terror, or of awe.

O nobly-born, when thou art driven [hither and thither] by the ever-moving wind of karma, thine intellect, having no object upon which to rest, will be like a feather tossed about by the wind, riding on the horse of breath. Ceaselessly and involuntarily wilt thou be wandering about. To all those who are weeping [thou wilt say], 'Here I am; weep not.' But they not hearing thee, thou wilt think, 'I am dead!' And again, at that time, thou wilt be feeling very miserable. Be not miserable in that way.

There will be a grey twilight-like light, both by night and by day, and at all times. In that kind of Intermediate State thou wilt be either for one, two, three, four, five, six, or seven weeks, until the forty-ninth day. It hath been said that ordinarily the miseries of the Sidpa Bardo are experienced for about twenty-one days; but, because of the determining influence of *karma*, a fixed period is not assured.

More than a few people continue to wander in this state for months or even years.

The Book of the Dead continues:

> O nobly-born, at about that time, the fierce wind of *karma*, terrific and hard to endure, will drive thee [onwards], from behind, in dreadful gusts.

> O nobly-born, at that time, at bridge-heads, in temples, by *stupas* of eight kinds, thou wilt rest a little while, but thou wilt not be able to remain there very long, for thine intellect hath been separated from thine [earth-plane] body. Because of this inability to loiter, thou oft-times wilt feel perturbed and vexed and panic-stricken. At times, thy Knower will be dim; at times, fleeting and incoherent. Thereupon this thought will occur to thee, 'Alas! I am dead! What shall I do?' and because of such thought the Knower will become saddened and the heart chilled, and thou wilt experience infinite misery of sorrow. Since thou canst not rest in any one place, and feel impelled to go on, think not of various things, but allow the intellect to abide in its own [unmodified] state.

> As to food, only that which hath been dedicated to thee can be partaken of by thee, and no other food. As to friends at this time, there will be no certainty.

> These are the indications of the wandering about on the *Sidpa Bardo* of the mental body. At

the time, happiness and misery will depend upon *karma*.

Thou wilt see thine own home, the attendants, relatives, and the corpse, and think 'Now I am dead! What shall I do?' And being oppressed with intense sorrow, the thought will occur to thee, 'O what would I not give to possess a body!' And so thinking, thou wilt be wandering hither and thither seeking a body.

The Plain of Death

After a long while, as though drawn by a magnet, the dead person finally turns in the direction he is meant to go.

He heads towards the place where the dead assemble.

People who understand the death process and are facing it openly usually arrive at this destination more quickly than people who don't, whereas people who are filled with vengefulness and attachment can take a very long time to reach it. But, no matter how long it takes, this is where all dead people ultimately end up.

As he begins to travel towards this next stage in the process the dead person starts to recognize what is going on. He begins to remember bits and pieces about the awful ordeal he is about to endure. The memories freeze his soul with fear.

"Oh God, here I am again."

He starts to tremble all over and sinks even further into despair. An irresistible force is compelling him onwards. Onwards to *that place*.

Now, sometimes a person is so terrified that he fights as hard as he can to avoid the inevitable. He may even manage to break free from the force for a little while, to flee in another direction. But this only increases his suffering. Ultimately, his efforts will come to nothing. He will eventually end up going to *that place*.

For some people *that place* seems like it's very far away. For others it seems as close as their backyards.

That place.

The one that's called *the Plain of Death*.

The Plain of Death is a vast, wide-open plateau that stretches as far as the eye can see. The sound of the wind whistles through the barren branches of the stunted scraggly bushes that dot the landscape. Hardly any grass is growing on the infinite expanse of bleak gray earth.

There is no day or night, nor a visible sun. The area is illuminated by weak rays of light that filter through hazy mists like twilight in autumn.

Now and then, a chill wind blows up from between our dead person's legs. It comes from the network of crevices that split the ground. One of these fissures has become a bottomless abyss. The abyss extends endlessly off into the distance.

He looks into the abyss but all he can see is eerie mist and fog swirling around down below. Every once in a while the abyss emits a blast of icy air.

He looks across the abyss, but he can't see anything on

the other side. The far banks are shrouded in the same mist and fog.

But then, every once in a while, a breeze will part the mist to reveal, just for a moment, a range of verdant green mountains surprisingly close to where he is standing. These mountains are topped by a brilliant blue sky so bright that it dazzles his eyes.

So this is what it's like, where he finds himself. On the Plain of Death.

The Plain of Death is the end of our world, the farthest outpost of our dimension. It is where we have to go to enter the next one.

Clusters of the Dead

There is a vast assembly of dead people gathered on this plain. Their bodies look like shadows. They are not solid but mirage-like, gray and semi-transparent. Some of the bodies have skeletons showing through their skin. Others look pretty much the way they did when they were alive.

There are all kinds of people here. There are males and females of all ages, spanning every social stratum. There are thousands, millions, of them, more than one can count. They are all crowded together cheek by jowl into an enormous group.

Some of these beings are wearing clothes, some are

half-dressed, and some are completely naked.

Some people lie prostrate, exhausted, on the ground. The bodies of these souls look like outlines that have been filled with transparent gelatin. They don't look like they have any bones at all.

This crowd of dead humanity is not quiet. It is howling, yelling and screaming in a cacophony of pain. Many of the people are chanting religious protocols in unison. Some are intoning mantras, and some are reciting sutras. Some are spewing foul language: profanity, curses, hateful and bitter invective.

The people spontaneously cluster together in likeminded groups. Just because you were related to someone on earth doesn't necessarily mean you will get together here. If your karmic level is very different from someone you used to be connected to, even if that person was your spouse or a member of your immediate family, you probably won't meet up with them in this dimension. Even if you both happen to be there at the same time you won't be able to see each other. Dead people tend to gravitate to beings with whom they share ideas and beliefs. For this reason, the clusters of people who used to belong to the same major religion are huge.

The din coming from the entire assembly is loud enough to move heaven and earth, but, oddly enough, the sound of the collective voice contains no reverberation. And so it is absorbed silently into space.

The earthly name for the abyss that spans the Plain of Death is 'the river of the three streams,' but the deceased call it 'the valley of hell'.

The dead person is now confronted with a great task.

In order to continue on his journey, he has to leap across the abyss and reach the other side.

For on the other side of the abyss is the realm, or land, of transition.

And it is intuitively clear to him that the only way to find relief from the torment he is experiencing is to reach the haven of the other side.

There is no place over here, at the end of this world, to find even a moment's rest. The only possibility of comfort is over there.

He has to jump. There is nothing else left to do.

He looks around. He sees people balanced on the edge of the precipice who are getting ready to make the leap. Occasionally he hears a cheer go up from the crowd. But the cheer soon turns into a wail of mourning.

A person jumps into the air. Not having a physical body, the person is so light that the breeze lifts him easily and he begins to sail across. But then something happens and he seems to stop in mid-air. Suddenly, without warning, he drops straight down, like a rock, and disappears completely into the mists below.

The person falls into a swift flowing river that is at the bottom of the abyss, and this river flows into the depths of the hell realms.

This happens to one person after another.

The invisible weight that stops these people from flying over the abyss is the negative karma that they collected when they were alive.

And the weight is not only the karma of bad deeds. It is also the karma of negative thoughts. Bad thoughts act as weight in people's minds to rob them of buoyancy.

Not having a body doesn't necessarily leave one weightless. Negative mental constructs like attachment and resentment are as heavy as lead.

The only people who are able to effortlessly leap across the abyss are people who have attained liberation from all their negative karma and achieved the state of emptiness.

Shakyamuni Buddha spent his whole life teaching us how to do this.

Shakyamuni Buddha left behind specific instructions on how to leap from the precipice and make it over to the other side of the abyss. These are recorded in the Agama Sutras. He taught us a method that is known as 'the 7 systems and the 37 practices for attaining Buddhahood'.

About the Hell Realms

Loud commotions erupt here and there.

Groups of people surround leaders who they feel have misled them. They are yelling at them, complaining bitterly and vociferously that they were tricked and cheated. The masses have rounded up the leaders and their aides and are pushing them to the edge of the cliff, where they are losing their balance and falling off into the abyss below.

One such leader cowers on the edge of the precipice, too scared to jump. The leader's constituents come over and lift him up and throw him bodily into the void. This person is so full of hot air and so fat from feasting off the adulation of his constituents that he drops straight down into the abyss, before he has gone even three feet.

The river that lies at the bottom of the chasm splits into three streams. Each of these leads into one of the hell realms. The nearest stream is the one that flows into the scariest of the hells. This is the one he is sucked into.

And over there is a famous priest. He is so sure of his destiny that he kicks off from the edge of the chasm with great confidence. He ascends high into the air as his flock raises its voice in prayer and admiration.

But then a strong wind gusts up from below and blows the priest straight back to where he started.

He tries to leap off the cliff again and again. Each time he is blown back to edge of the chasm. He doesn't fall into the abyss, but he also isn't making it across.

Now this gentleman is someone who behaved correctly throughout his lifetime. He cut all desire and didn't create any bad karma. But he had absolutely no concern for anyone else's salvation besides his own. His prayers were selfish. All he wanted to do was die a peaceful death and go to heaven.

And now he doesn't have enough merit to get across to the other side.

Because this man didn't behave badly and didn't have negative thoughts, and because his mind did attain a certain realization of emptiness, he is able to lift off easily into the air but he hasn't collected enough virtue to propel himself forward. Virtue is the thrust.

He finally becomes exhausted from trying to leap across the abyss and wanders off, disappearing somewhere into the distance.

Many people who take off from the edge of the abyss are filled with pride and confidence in what they accomplished here on earth. They were very rich, or powerful, or smart, or they were a famous artist, or a sports celebrity, or a movie star. Their egos are inflated, and they are sure they will have no trouble breezing over the chasm. They all fall out of the sky like rocks. They have finally met up with a situation where money or power or talent or popularity won't do them any good. Their egos can actually hinder them by acting like lead weights attached to the body.

Over there is a great magnate who amassed an enormous fortune during his lifetime. Late in life he experienced an enormous change of heart, and started giving away a tremendous amount of money to charitable causes. He began to meditate and had a certain realization of emptiness. He came to the intellectual understanding that life and death and heaven and hell are nothing more than reflections of the mind. Now that he has died, he feels very put upon that he should have to face this obstacle. He goes to the edge of the abyss, lets out a concentrated shout, and takes off into the unknown. He immediately drops down into the abyss.

Now it's true that he worked very hard late in life to extinguish desire and to learn to meditate, and that he did attain some degree of realization. But, in the meantime, he forgot about all the people who he hurt when he was young and making his money. There are a lot of people who have grudges against this man and who bear him ill will.

I spoke before about the mental weight that people

can carry. But this weight does not have to be one that is self-created in your own mind. It can also be projected onto you from the minds of other people. And this fellow didn't realize that he was carrying around a ton of it.

Some religious sects teach that one can attain liberation by concentrating intensively on paradise at the moment of death. However, I find that in practice there are very few people who can accomplish this.

But, what I do see is that people can be lifted over the abyss through the prayers of those who are still alive. Every now and again one of the exhausted souls who has been lying on the ground will float up into the air and take off over the abyss. His descendants have dedicated the merit of a memorial service to his advancement, and this has given him the power he needs to move forward into the transitional realm.

When this happens, the other dead people who are around him just stare at him vacantly as he floats by.

There are so many different kinds of people here. Some of them are atheists or materialists. These people really don't have a clue. They form their own groups, standing around frozen in place, totally bewildered. They don't have any idea what's going on.

Eventually people start to become increasingly frantic and hysterical. There is no hypothetical deity who is going to rescue them. The whole thing begins to look like a scene out of hell.

Every once in a while a figure flies by high above.

There is a faint aura emanating from these flying figures. Who might they be?

They are beings who have attained one of the 'four

stages of enlightenment'.

Beings who have become saints through actualizing practices leading to liberation like 'the 37 practices of enlightenment' or 'the cultivation of three merits' that Shakyamuni Buddha taught are able to fly high above the abyss. These beings are flying so high that they by-pass the transitional realm on the other side and go directly into the spiritual realms up ahead.

When the people on the plain notice a shadowy figure gliding above, they stretch out their arms in supplication, leap off the ground, and try to grab hold of the saint to 'hitch a ride'. When the people are jumping up and down like this they look like a hoard of agitated grasshoppers.

Now and then, small groups break off from the crowd and go running away from the abyss. It looks like they are trying to find another way out of the situation.

The Four Stages of *Shravaka* Sainthood

The 'four stages of enlightenment' of the *shravaka*, or practitioner, are:

> *Srotapanna*
> *Sakridagamin*
> *Anagamin*
> *Arhat*

The *srotapanna* stage of attainment is also known as that of the 'streamwinner', meaning that the practitioner has entered the stream of sainthood and has attained the first stage of enlightenment. This sage is also referred to as a 'seven-time returner'. This means the practitioner will be reborn from the spiritual realm into this world seven times in order to accumulate good karma before he enters the Buddha realm.

The traditional interpretation of this term is that it literally means the individual will be reborn seven times as a human being. But I have clairvoyantly come to understand that it doesn't necessarily take seven. The process can be over in three or four times. Furthermore, it doesn't always mean birth in the form of a human being. This sage may be reborn once or twice as a human being, and then take his next rebirth into the spirit world from which he will visit this world, proceed to perform good deeds, and then return once again to the spiritual realm.

The *sakridagamin* is one stage above the *srotapanna*. This sage is also referred to as a 'once returner'. He will be reborn just one more time from the spiritual realm into this world of desire.

The difference between a 'seven-time returner' and a 'once returner' is that the 'once returner' will actually be reborn as a human being. As a general rule, while on earth this person will either be a saint or a great humanitarian. And then he or she will proceed directly to the Buddha realm. This is why this stage is called a 'once returner'.

An *anagamin* is a 'non-returner'. Once this sage leaves this world of desire he will not come back again. He will enter into the spiritual realms, and from there directly enter the Buddha realm.

An arhat is the same as a buddha, so needs no further commentary.

Shakyamuni Buddha taught that a person can attain these four stages, become a sage, and enter the Buddha realm by actualizing the 37 practices for attaining enlightenment or by cultivating the three merits.

The Buddha summarizes this teaching in the *Osetsu Sutra* of the *Samyukta Agama*:

> A disciple must practice mindfulness, right efforts, the psychic powers, the roots, the excellent powers, the factors, and the path (of the means of attaining Buddhahood) in order to attain taintless liberation (perfect Buddhahood).

Further, in the *Sankuyobon Sutra* of the *Ekottara Agama*, the Buddha teaches that:

> This is the path of the three merits. They are of untold goodness and will lead you over time to the state of Nirvana. What are these three? Cultivate merit at the feet of the Tathagata. This merit is of untold benefit. Cultivate merit where the right Dharma is being maintained. This merit is of untold benefit. Cultivate merit among the Sangha. This merit is of untold benefit. Brethren, the cultivation of the path of three merits is untold. Cutting through the five chains of the lower world (*pañca-avara-bhagiya-samyojanani*) leads the disciple from the stage of *srotapanna* to the stage of *anagamin*. This is the path of merit that will lead you to the realm of Nirvana.

Taintless liberation is perfect Buddhahood (Nirvana). One can enter it in this world when one still has a physical body or after death. The Buddha taught that these four stages of sainthood, in particular, are most important to attaining the perfected Buddhahood of the Buddha realm that one enters into after death.

Of course, if you have not achieved liberation from karma while you are alive, you will not attain a state of liberated Buddhahood after you die.

But the state of one's liberation or lack thereof on earth is directly connected to one's state in the afterworld. The Buddha made this very clear.

"I'll Do Anything to Get a Body"

Who else might one encounter here on the Plain of Death?

There are some people who are even unhappier that the ones we've seen so far.

Remember I mentioned there was a group of people running away from the Plain of Death?

Where were they going?

As it turns out, they went rushing back to places where they still had attachments, locations where they had 'left their minds'.

At first these people were just as focused on making it over to the transitional realm as everybody else. But as they began to despair of ever accomplishing that and grew increasingly fearful of falling into the valley of hell their minds became obsessed with returning to someplace familiar.

One consequence of no longer having a physical body is the ability to rapidly transfer one's mind, as is, from one place to another. This is what these individuals did.

They went back to someplace familiar. Maybe to the spot where they died. Or to where someone they are attached to is located.

But as soon as they get there they realize that it is not what they expected. It's awful.

When you don't have a physical body there is no place for your mind to ground itself. The mind becomes extremely unstable, subject to radical fluctuations. It spins out thoughts at enormous speed and turns into a tormented whirlpool of negative emotions, of jealousy, remorse, hatred, pain, and attachment.

Being back in the old place just intensifies the person's pain. They keep moving, looking for someplace, anyplace, where they can find some peace and rest.

As they move away from the known environment, they find themselves in yet a worse situation.

They wander into a realm of terrifying transformations that never stop. Nights are pitch black and filled with the ravages of tornadoes, weird sounds, blinding blizzards, and typhoons. Daytime is a constant barrage of blistering heat and hot winds. To make matters worse, the dead person is haunted by demonic visions. Constant hallucinations. They are absolutely alone. No one else is there.

They certainly haven't found any peace or comfort.

They may have made it back to where they came from but it's nothing like it was.

This compels them to keep on moving, restlessly. Our dead soul has now become one of the wandering spirits that I mentioned before.

Wandering spirits are haunted by all the feelings they can't bear to remember from their previous life, and the one before that, and the one before that, from 10 or 20 lifetimes ago. All their bad deeds and evil thoughts and passionate attachments are magnified 10 or 100 times and have turned around to attack them. Every bad thing they ever experienced comes back to them. Imagine if they had killed someone or been murdered themselves or had a horrible sexual relationship. All those feelings come back, accompanied by uncontrollable visions.

Finally their agony reaches a point where the person truly can't stand it any longer. This is when he or she becomes desperate to get a body.

"God, this hurts so much. I can't bear it. I have to get back into a physical body, any body, no matter what it takes."

The person is frantic to find a body in which to ground his or her tormented mind.

The person is running around thinking, "I've got to get myself a body. I don't care what kind of being I'm reborn as, I've just got to find some kind of body as soon as possible."

Sometimes they are compelled to enter the body of someone to whom they are attached.

This state of mind is described in *The Tibetan Book of the Dead*:

(Oh, nobly-born. At that time,) the visions of males and females in union will appear.

If [about] to be born as a male, the feeling of itself being a male dawneth upon the Knower, and a feeling of intense hatred towards the father and of jealousy and attraction towards the mother is begotten. If [about] to be born as a female, the feeling of itself being a female dawneth upon the Knower, and a feeling of intense hatred towards the mother and of intense attraction and fondness towards the father is begotten.

(Through these feelings) one entereth into the womb.

This is how a person is reborn.

When a living being can't stand the pain of life he or she commits suicide and dies. When a dead person can't stand the pain of death he or she reincarnates and is reborn.

The Rebirth of a Saint

At this point, the reader may be quite confused because the description of Katsugoro's rebirth doesn't quite jibe with the above information.

Indeed, that's because they are different.

Katsugoro wasn't an ordinary human being.

He was a streamwinner, someone who had attained the first stage of sainthood. We find evidence of this when he says, "I am a buddha (*Nono-sama*): therefore please be kind to me." This isn't something that an ordinary child would ever say.

Also, he has a sage there to guide him. This is further proof that he was a streamwinner. Because a streamwinner is a beginning, or novice, sage, a more experienced sage is often sent along to guide them. (When we become streamwinners we will be met by sage guides who will lead us across that abyss.)

When streamwinners are born into this world they often return to the spiritual dimension while they are still children. As you might expect, they easily re-enter the spiritual realm because they have pure hearts that have not yet been tainted by worldly defilements.

As Tozo in his previous lifetime, Katsugoro died when he was six years old. I imagine that the next time he comes back into this world it may be in the form of spirit, and then after that he'll ascend to the level of *sakrdagamin*.

When he reaches that stage he will be reborn once more into this world as a saint or a humanitarian, after which he will return to the spiritual dimension. Then he will never return to this world again.

You may be surprised to learn that there are streamwinner children in our midst, close to us. A family that loses one of these children and goes on to specially honor the child's spirit will see an increase in its good fortune. It is most important that we take very good care of our children.

Finally, I would like to end this book with the last words that Shakyamuni Buddha uttered:

"Indeed, bhikkhus, I declare this to you: It is in the nature of all formations to dissolve. Attain perfection through diligence."

Afterword

At the beginning of this year (1993) there was an interview with two internationally recognized scientists published in the Asahi Newspaper. One was Ken'ichi Fukui, winner of the Nobel Prize for chemistry in 1981, and the other was Osamu Hayaishi, director of the Osaka Bioscience Institute.

It made for fascinating reading. Here is an excerpt. Under the subtitle "The Mind and the Brain," Dr. Hayaishi said:

> The turn of the century saw great developments in the field of biology. By mid-century, we had unlocked the structure of the gene and made major advances in the field of genetic engineering. So, we ask, what is the major challenge facing us in the 21st century? Ninety-nine out of a hundred people would answer that the most compelling and important issue that remains is the molecular biological and biophysical functioning of the brain.

The brain has the most complex functions of any biological organ that God created.

We are now at the point, as noted by Dr. Fukui, where we are gradually beginning to gain an understanding of sensory functions like sight, hearing, smell, and taste on a biophysical and enzymatic level.

But we still have many questions about the overall functioning of the brain and its relationship to mind, or, if you like, soul. Is there a spiritual dimension that is distinct from the brain, a dimension that has no form? Or can all such phenomena be explained from the standpoints of chemistry and physics? I believe that we scientists do have the wherewithal to answer these questions.

He later says:

Lately I sometimes think about what is going to happen to me after I die. I've entertained the possibility of my soul going somewhere else, but I believe that I am going to disappear. I don't believe that my spirit is going to rise up and be looking down from heaven.

Dr. Fukui responds:

I absolutely agree with you. I believe that the self exists as long as there is a consciousness to confirm its existence. The human life span of maybe 50 years is nothing more than an instant in the flow of universal time. Taking this to the extreme, we can say that the individual is only a specific, momentary point in the space of the vastness of the universe. For all we know, this is true for the whole body of the human race as well. I think of this as 'the cyclical flow of birth and death'. Arising and cessation flow along together. This may sound like a Buddhist concept, but is not religious in nature.

Dr. Hayaishi responds:

Whether we refer to it as mind or as consciousness, the phenomenon is ultimately a function of the brain. When the brain is damaged, consciousness disappears. When one dies, there is nothing left but matter.

Both of these scientists are clearly on the side of the brain-only theorists. I have nothing relevant to say about that here (having already addressed it in the body of this book). However, both of them do use the word 'consciousness' and I would like to say a little bit about that.

Dr. Fukui says, "I believe that the self exists as long as there is a consciousness to confirm its existence." Dr. Hayaishi asserts, "Whether we refer to it as mind or as consciousness, the phenomenon is ultimately a function of the brain. When the brain is damaged, consciousness disappears. When one dies, there is nothing left but matter."

Shakyamuni Buddha taught that after death there

arises a 'body of consciousness'. In other words, mind or consciousness is the only thing that continues to exist after the physical body is gone. In Tibetan Buddhism they refer to this as the 'mental body' (*manomayakaya*).

I think it will be truly marvelous when this and similar phenomena are elucidated by the disciplines of biochemistry and biophysics.

"I believe that the self exists as long as there is a consciousness to confirm its existence."

I remember hearing almost the exact same sentiment when, some time ago, I was having a discussion about reincarnation with a well-known Catholic priest from the Vatican.

He reasoned, "Even if we posit the existence of reincarnation, if the self that I am now comes back as a completely different person (in that I become a person whose consciousness is different than the consciousness I presently have), then we couldn't really term it reincarnation as such."

I asked him this question.

"May I ask if you have dreams?"

"Yes, I do."

"Have you ever had a bad dream in which you were being chased by something that frightened you?"

"Yes, I have."

"When that happens, is the you that gets scared the same you that is present here now in a state of clear consciousness? I'm sure that even when dreaming you sometimes experience a clear sense of yourself, but aren't there times when you're not quite sure of who you are, you just know that you are being chased by something terrifying which fills you with dread?"

He thought about this for a moment.

"I can't say that I haven't had this happen."

"That's what I'd expect. I've had the same thing happen myself. It's not clear who or where I am, or maybe I'm even a completely different person, but something frightening is after me. A few times my moans and shouts were so loud that my family had to wake me up."

He nodded silently.

"That's what I mean. The self that is born as someone somewhere in the next world is essentially, always, your 'self'. It is the same 'self' that experiences your suffering, your pain, and that experiences your joy. The consciousness that will cognize the person you will become in your next reincarnation is always your 'self'."

This priest was definitely not about to acknowledge the existence of reincarnation, but my argument left him with a perplexed expression on his face and he didn't try to argue with me any further.

Both Dr. Fukui and Dr. Hayashi subscribe to the view of the brain-only theorists but, I must say, I was deeply impressed by the fact that neither of them made the subsequent deduction that "so-called spirit is just superstition." This indicates to me that they are true scientists.

Let me end with a statement from a scientist I quoted in the body of this book, the man for whom I have such deep respect, Professor Penfield.

Indeed, no scientist, by virtue of his science, has the right to pass judgement on the faiths by which men live and die. We can only set out the data about the brain, and present the physiological hypotheses that are relevant to what the mind does.

May 20, 1993

Bibliography

Alajouanine, T.; "Aphasia and Artistic Realization,"*Brain*, 71:229–241, 1948.

Gershom, Rabbi Yonasson, *Beyond the Ashes*, A.R.E.Press, Virginia Beach, Virginia, 1992.

Hearn, Lafcadio, *Gleanings in Buddha-Fields*, Houghton, Mifflin, and Co., Boston, 1897.

Kiriyama, Seiyu, *Kanno shiko—Reiteki baiohoronikusu no jidai*, Hirakawa Shuppan, Tokyo, 1984.

——, *Henshin no genri*, Bun'ichi Shuppan, Tokyo, 1971; Kadokawa Bunko, Tokyo, 1975.

——, *Mikkyo: Chonoryoku no himitsu*, Hirakawa Shuppan, Tokyo, 1972.

Koestler, Arthur, *Janus: A Summing Up*, Random House, New york, 1978.

Luria, A.R., L.S.Tsvetkova, and D.S.Futer:"Aphasia in a Composer,"*Journal of the Neurological Sciences*, 2:288–292, 1965.

Penfieled, Wilder, *The Mystery of the Mind*, Princeton University Press, Princeton, New Jersey, 1974.

Stevenson, Ian, *Children Who Remember Previous Lives*, University Press of Virginia, Charlottesville, Virginia, 1987.

Szondi, L., *Unmei e no chosen(Triebpalhologie)*, translated by Ryuzo Satake, Kanazawa Bunko, Tokyo, 1973.

The Tibetan Book of the Dead, compiled and edited by W.Y.Evans-Wentz, Oxford University Press, London, 1927.

Yamatori, Atsushi, *No kara mita kokoro*, NHK Books, Nihon Hoso Shuppan Kyokai, Tokyo, 1985.

Yoro, Takeshi, *Yuinoron*, Seidosha, Tokyo, 1989.

ABOUT THE AUTHOR

Seiyu KIRIYAMA

Founder of Agon Shu Buddhist Association;
Professor Emeritus of Peking University;
Professor Emeritus of Zhongshan University;
Professor Emeritus of the National Buddhist
Seminary of China (Buddhist College);
Member of the Board of Directors, University of
San Francisco;
Professor Emeritus and Honorary Doctor of Philosophy,
National University of Mongolia;
Honorable Doctorate Degree in Journalism and Mass Communication,
Thammasat University;
Honorary Fellow of School of Oriental and African Studies,
University of London;
Visiting Professor and Honorary Dean of the Nyingmapa
Tibetan Buddhist College;
Honorary Archbishop of the Siam Sect of Sri Lankan Buddhism;
Title of the Highest Rank of the Clergy of Myanmar Buddhism;
Director of the Chinese International Qigong Research Center (Beijing);
Honorary Member of the Dutch Treat Club, New York;
Honorary Ninth Rank, Japanese Go Association.

Author of 56 books,
including "Agon Buddhism as the Source of
'Shamatha (Tranquillity) and Vipashyanā (Insight)',"
"21st Century: The Age of *Sophia*,"
"You Have Been Here Before: Reincarnation,"
"The Wisdom of the *Goma* Fire Ceremony,"
"The Marvel of Spiritual Transformation,"
"Sacred Buddhist Fire Ceremony for World Peace 2001,"
and "The *Heart Sutra* Meditation,"
and the soon-to-be-released
"The Practitioner's Guide to Agon Buddhism."

AGON SHU OFFICE ADDRESSES

Main Temple
Shakazan Daibodai-ji
Omine-cho, Yamashina-ku,
Kyoto City 607-8471,
JAPAN

Kanto Main Office
Agon Shu Kanto Betsuin
4-14-15 Mita, Minato-ku,
Tokyo 108-8318,
JAPAN
Tel. 81-3-3769-1931

Kansai Main Office
Agon Shu Kansai So-honbu
Jingumichi Agaru, Sanjodori,
Higashiyama-ku,
Kyoto City 605-0031,
JAPAN
Tel. 81-75-761-1141

Hawaii Branch Office
Agon Mission of Hawaii
The Tradewinds B-1-C,
1720 Ala Moana Blvd.,
Honolulu, Hawaii 96815,
U.S.A.
Tel. 1-808-949-4652

Europe Branch Office
Agon Shu UK
3 Queen Square, London WC1N 3AU,
England, UK
Tel. 44-20-7278-1988

Brazil Branch Office
Associacao Budista Agon Shu
Rua Getulio Vargas Filho,
131-Cidade Vargas,
CEP: 04318-030-Sao Paulo-SP,
BRASIL
Tel. 55-11-5011-2102

Canada Branch office
Agon Shu Canada Buddhist
Association
1255 Yonge St., Suite 302,
Toronto, Ontario M4T 1W6,
CANADA
Tel. 1-416-922-1272

Taipei Main Office
Agon Shu Taipei Honbu
1F.No.27-6, Sec.2, Chung-Cheng
East Rd., Tamshui, Taipei,
TAIWAN
Tel. 886-2-2808-4601

Kaohsiung Branch Office
Agon Shu Takao Shibu
No.975 Jung Hua 5th Rd.,
Chian Jen Sec., Kaohsiung,
TAIWAN
Tel. 886-7-537-2002

You Have Been Here Before:
Reincarnation
君は誰れの輪廻転生か【英語版】

2000年11月1日　第1版第1刷発行
2005年 3月1日　第1版第3刷発行

著　者……桐山靖雄
　　　　　Ⓒ 2000 by Seiyu Kiriyama
訳　者……ランディ・ブラウン
発行者……森真智子
発行所……株式会社平河出版社
　　　　　〒108-0073東京都港区三田3-4-8
　　　　　電話03(3454)4885　FAX 03(5484)1660
　　　　　振替00110-4-117324
装　幀……谷村彰彦
印刷所……日本写真印刷株式会社
用紙店……中庄株式会社